AF268716

Baptized!
Why Did I Get Wet?

Kirkland M. Rite

First Printing: 2026

Eternal Kingdom International Publishing, LLC

LIBRARY OF CONGRESS

LCCN: 2026939386

ISBN- 978-1-968815-16-5 - Paperback

ISBN- 978-1-968815-18-9 - eBook

ISBN- 978-1-968815-19-6 – Case Laminate

A Note from EKI Publishing:

This book is part of a larger Kingdom reading pathway developed through EKI Books. These works are designed to help readers grow from foundational truths into mature Kingdom life, moving from repentance, identity, and inner restoration into transformation, body life, leadership, and deeper revelation. While each book may be read on its own, together they form a broader discipleship framework.

The EKI Reading Pathway

Foundations
- *Repent: U-Turns Required* - Kirkland M. Rite *(Coming Soon)*
- *Baptized: Why Did I Get Wet* - Kirkland M. Rite
- *Sozo: What Am I Saved From* - Kirkland M. Rite *(Coming Soon)*

Identity
- *Unchained* - Kirkland M. Rite

Discern the Times & Understand His Voice
- *The Language of Dreams (title forthcoming)* - David S. Webb *(Coming Soon)*
- *I Am the Sign* - Kirkland M. Rite *(Coming Soon)*

Restore the Inner Life
- *Soul Made Whole* - David S. Webb *(Coming Soon)*

Grow Into the New Nature
- *The New Nature Series* - Kirkland M. Rite *(Coming Soon)*

Walk in Kingdom Life
- *Walking in the Kingdom* - David S. Webb *(Coming Soon)*
- *Escape the Shame of Babylon* - David S. Webb
- *The Unique Factor* - David S. Webb

Build Within the Body
- *Building the King Through the Local Church* - David S. Webb
- *Building the Temple to Hold the Glory* - David S. Webb
- *Every Joint Supplieth* - Kirkland M. Rite *(Coming Soon)*

Multiply and Lead
- *Spiritual Fathers (title forthcoming)* - David S. Webb *(Coming Soon)*
- *The Elisha Mandate* - Kirkland M. Rite *(Coming Soon)*

Go Deeper
- *A Gospel of Convicts* - Kirkland M. Rite *(Coming Soon)*
- *The Covenant of Salt* - Kirkland M. Rite *(Coming Soon)*

Foundational and Supplemental Works
- *The Noah Generation* - Kevin Rice
- *Cultivating the New Nature: Growing into the Full Stature of Christ* - Kevin Rice

Companion Resources
- *Values for Living Above and Beyond* - Kevin Rice *(Coming Soon)*

Workbooks and Study Guides - EKI Publishing Team *(Coming Soon)*

Other Works by Kirkland M. Rite:

- _Unchained: Freed to be His Treasure_ EKI Publishing 2025

- _Baptized: Why Did I Get Wet_ EKI Publishing 2026

- _Sozo: What Am I Saved From?_ EKI Publishing 2026

And there are three that bear witness on earth:
the Spirit, the water, and the blood; and these
three agree as one.

-   1 John 5:8

Dedication:

This book is dedicated to those who stepped into the water before they understood everything - and discovered that obedience often walks ahead of explanation.

To the ones who were washed not because they had every answer, but because the Word had awakened them and the river was waiting.

To the pastors who kept the water ready. To the parents who stood dripping and smiling. To the witnesses - seen and unseen - who knew heaven was paying attention long before the crowd was.

And to the Lamb, whose blood gave the water a voice, whose Spirit still breathes where hearts are yielded, and whose obedience turned a river into a doorway.

Kirkland M. Rite

Contents

18

Prelude

Cold Water, Warm Spirit

When I got baptized, I was twelve years old - and the water could have frozen a penguin.

Our church, a medium-sized congregation of about 150 souls, sat on a hill where the winter wind had a bad habit of finding every crack in the siding. The baptistry was built right against the outside wall, which meant the water was roughly the same temperature as a January creek. No heater. No bubbles. Just the promise of obedience - and hypothermia.

I remember changing into the white robe in that cold little side room, shivering, nervous, and trying to solve the great theological mystery every twelve-year-old boy faces at baptism: *Do you leave your underwear on, or take it off?* Nobody told me that part in Sunday school.

For weeks, I had wrestled with the decision to be baptized. I knew the Lord had been dealing with my heart, and I knew what the preacher had said. I thought I understood it. In my young mind, baptism was like pressing "save" on my soul so I wouldn't lose my progress in heaven's game.

But deep down, I felt something bigger stirring.

From the time I could remember, I knew the Lord was real. I talked to Him in the woods, whispered prayers when I was alone. He was the Friend who never walked away (Proverbs 18:24b). He was near to me long before I had words for what He was doing in my heart. I just did not yet understand that baptism was not only about getting wet. It was about answering Him.

I stepped out of the changing room into the narrow hallway that led to the steps of the baptistry. My dad stood nearby, smiling, proud, a little misty-eyed. I took a deep breath, and when my foot touched that water, I knew I would remember it for the rest of my life.

It was *cold* as death.

Not "chilly." Not "brisk." It was the kind of cold that shocks your soul and makes you question your life choices. Each step down felt like walking into an ice bath of destiny. My breath came out in short bursts. My teeth began a worship service of their own, chattering in perfect rhythm.

When I reached the bottom, the water hit my chest, and my breathing stopped. The pastor looked down at me with a kind smile and said the words I had heard him say to so many others.

I pinched my nose, closed my eyes, and braced for impact.

Then, *down I went.*

For a split second, everything froze. The water swallowed me whole, and the world went silent. It felt like eternity wrapped in two seconds. When I came back up, gasping, shivering, blinking water from my eyes, I was still alive.

My dad was crying, the church was shouting, I did not come up glowing. I did not hear angels. I did not float three inches above the baptistry.

I just felt still. Peaceful.

Settled in a way I did not know how to explain.

That matters to me now, because not every real moment with God arrives like thunder. Some arrive like still water after the splash. Some do not overwhelm you emotionally; they anchor you. They do not make you feel wild. They make you know you answered something real.

They handed me a towel, and I ran back to the changing room faster than Peter running to the tomb (John 20:3–4). I dried off, threw my clothes back on, and emerged to find my dad still smiling through tears.

I did not understand much that day. I did not know the history behind baptism. I did not know how many arguments Christians would build around it. I did not know how much confusion, tradition, pride, fear, and hope people would drag to the edge of the water with them.

I only knew this: something in me had answered God.

That day stayed with me.

It stayed with me through years of reading Scripture, years of hearing sermons, years of watching people argue over formulas, methods, meanings, and motives. It stayed with me while I watched some people treat baptism like a photo opportunity, others like a denominational badge, and still others like a ritual too dangerous to question. Through all of it, the same question kept returning to me:

Why did I get wet?

Not just why did I step into the water that day, but what was God saying through it? Why does water keep showing up in the story of Scripture? Why does baptism stand at the crossing of obedience, identity, witness, cleansing, burial, beginning, and belonging? Why has the church managed to make something so vivid feel so small - or so complicated?

This book is my attempt to walk back to the water and ask that question honestly.

Not as a salesman for tradition. Not as a collector of religious phrases. Not as a man trying to turn water into magic. And not as a man pretending the question is simple just because people are used to hearing easy answers.

I am going back to the river.

Back to the witness. Back to the Word. Back to the place where obedience often arrives before explanation.

So if you have ever stepped into the water without fully knowing why, or if you have stood on the bank wondering whether there was more there than you had been told, come with me.

The water is cold. The question is honest. And I think the answer is bigger than most of us were taught.

Let's find out together *why we got wet.*

Chapter One

The Original Splash Zone

The first time water appears in Scripture, it doesn't whisper onto the page - it roars across it. Before there were stars, gardens, or even Adam, there was water. *"The Spirit of God moved upon the face of the waters."* (Genesis 1:2)

The text never tells us when water began. It simply *was there*. It waited - silent, ancient, and patient - for the voice of God to break the stillness. Light was commanded into being. Land was shaped from chaos. Seeds and stars were spoken into their places. But water was already waiting beneath the breath of God.

From the beginning, water was more than a substance; it was present where God was about to act. It stood beneath the Word (logos)[1] that called worlds into being (John 1:1-5; Colossians 1:16). It mirrored the heavens. And through ages yet to come, it would appear again - in floods, in rivers, and in baptisms — whenever God marked cleansing, crossing, or beginning.

Scripture later says, *"There are three that bear witness on earth: the Spirit, and the water, and the blood."* (1 John 5:8). Heaven keeps its purposes; earth carries the testimony — in soil, in stone, and in

---

[1] In this book, I use logos for the Word as God's declared truth, and rhema for that Word made living and present to the hearer. One is the seed spoken; the other is the seed awakened. For fuller definitions of logos and rhema, see Glossary of Terms and Chapter 8.

water. Water is never just scenery in God's story; it shows up wherever creation, cleansing, or beginning is taking place.

That's why the story of creation begins not with soil, but with depth. Water became the womb of the world, and the Spirit hovered over its surface, preparing to call life out of waiting. (1) [2] Before light ever touched the earth, water had already felt the movement of God's breath (Genesis 1:2-3). Not because water thinks or remembers on its own, but because God chose to work through it. Water could respond, reflect, and receive - but it could never redeem. Long before Calvary, it was already waiting for something greater than itself. Before there was form, there was flow - and God chose to move through it.

When God Speaks in Water

From the beginning, whenever God wanted to begin again, He spoke in water. When the world drowned in corruption, favor floated on an ark (Genesis 7–8; 1 Peter 3:20–21).(2) [3] When Israel groaned beneath Egypt, the sea opened like a door (Exodus 14; 1 Corinthians 10:1–2).(3) [4] When a new generation trembled at the edge of promise, the Jordan rolled back its waves (Joshua 3:15–17).

[2] Theodor, J and Albeck, C (1965) Midrash Bereshit Rabba: Mit kritischem Apparat und Kommentar. 2nd ed. 3 vols. Jerusalem: Wahrmann Books
[3] Rice, K. M. (2023) *The Noah Generation*, EKI Publishing, Crown City, Ohio
[4] Rice, K. M. (2023). *Cultivating the New Nature* EKI Publishing, Crown City, Ohio

Every story begins with the same sound - the rush of living water, the pulse of something being made new. God's voice still carries a current (Psalm 29:3-4). And when He speaks, what cannot remain is carried away. Yet even then, those waters could only do so much. They prepared, but they could not finish. They carried away what people could see, but they pointed ahead to something deeper still to come.

The Gospel According to the Creek

Where I live, the creek cuts through the holler like a scar with a memory. The people who live along its edge are good people - proud, poor, and resilient. Out here, the trash truck doesn't always make it past the gravel and the switchbacks. So folks do what they can. They burn what will burn, bury what won't, and make do with the rest.

When the rains come, they come hard and fast. The creek swells and rages, licking the edge of the forest and tearing away what was left on the banks. The ashes, the bottles, the scraps - all of it gets caught up in the muddy rush and carried down toward the river.

You'd think it would make a mess. But it doesn't. Somehow, when the flood recedes, the banks gleam clean again - slick with fresh clay, ready for summer grass. The water doesn't ask permission; it just comes. It rushes through every hidden corner, carrying away the remains of what people couldn't carry themselves.

Every time I see it, I think of baptism. I think of how water can make room for what comes next. The flood never condemns what it cleans (Romans 8:1). It moves through and makes room for what comes next.

Water of Preparation

Long before John the Baptist cried out in the wilderness, Jewish life already spoke the language of water. (4–6) [5] [6] [7] Stone steps descended into **mikva'ot** – quiet pools where people washed and prepared themselves to draw near.

Priests immersed themselves before entering the Temple (Exodus 29:4). Israel already knew that water belonged to cleansing and readiness.

Those immersions were not empty ritual; they were rehearsals. So when John lifted his voice at the Jordan- *"Repent, for the kingdom of heaven is at hand!"* (Matthew 3:2), the people understood. The call wasn't to ceremony, but to readiness (Isaiah 40:3)

---

[5] H. Danby Trans. (1933) *The Mishnah*, Oxford University Press
[6] Ferguson, E. (2009). *Baptism in the Early Church: History, Theology, and Liturgy in the First Five Centuries*. Eerdmans
[7] Neusner, J. (1973). *The Idea of Purity in Ancient Judaism*. Brill

The River That Still Calls

They came by the hundreds - farmers, soldiers, scholars, and sinners - wading into that river with trembling hearts and hopeful eyes. The current swirled around their ankles. The wilderness held its breath, whispering of freedom.

And then one day, Jesus came.

The sinless One stood shoulder to shoulder with sinners. The Creator stepped into the same river where others came confessing sin. He stepped into the river because obedience was being revealed in public, and the Father's will was being embraced in the earth (Matthew 3:15-17).

When He rose from the water, heaven opened. The Spirit descended like a dove, hovering over the water, as it did in Genesis. The Father's voice echoed over the river, just as it had in the beginning: *This is My beloved Son, in whom I am well pleased.* (Matthew 3:16–17).

In that moment, the witnesses agreed. The water received Him. The Spirit affirmed Him. And within Him flowed the blood that would soon speak for all mankind (1 John 5:8).

The Pattern of Water and Spirit

From Genesis to Jesus, the pattern never changed: Water and Spirit marked new beginnings. Creation began that way. Israel passed through it. Christ revealed it. And by the time baptism appears in the New Testament, it does not arrive as a strange new ritual, but inside a story God has been telling all along.

God never promised the water would be warm, only that it would change you. It's as if God was saying from the beginning, "This is how I work - through water and Spirit" (John 3:5; Titus 3:5). Long before anyone was baptized in a church, God was already speaking through water.

Reflection from the River

Water has always stood where God was making something visible. In Genesis, He moved over it. In Exodus, He made a way through it. In the Gospels, He stepped into it. Scripture does not give water the place of a savior. It gives it the place of a witness. That is why baptism does not feel dropped into the Bible from nowhere. It arrives inside a story already wet with beginnings.

Every flood, every crossing, every baptism, still whispers the same invitation: *"Come to the water. Let it carry what you can't."*

Scripture Index

- Genesis 1:2
- Genesis 7–8
- Exodus 14
- Exodus 29:4
- Joshua 3:15–17
- Leviticus 15
- Isaiah 40:3
- Isaiah 43:19
- Matthew 3:2
- Matthew 3:15–17
- John 3:5
- Titus 3:5

- 1 Corinthians 10:1–2
- 1 Peter 3:20–21
- Romans 6:3–4
- 2 Corinthians 5:17
- 2 Corinthians 5:21
- Ephesians 4:24
- Philippians 2:6–8
- 1 John 5:8

Chapter Two

The Mikvah: Where the Story Really Starts

The Ancient Pools

The story of baptism didn't start in the church. It started in the water.

Before John ever cried out in the wilderness, before the crowds gathered at the Jordan, there were quiet pools carved into stone. They were called *mikva'ot* - sacred baths built into courtyards, beside synagogues, and along the winding streets of Jerusalem. Archaeologists have found them everywhere - near the Temple Mount, in village homes, even along the pilgrim roads that led to the feasts.

Each mikvah had to be fed by *mayim chayim* - living water. (8) [8] Some rabbis accepted still pools, but stricter sects, such as the Essenes, insisted the water must move - rain, springs, or a stream.

Maybe that is why Scripture so often links cleansing with movement. What flows can cleanse; what is sealed off stagnates. The image reaches deeper than the body. Water in Scripture does not merely rinse surfaces; it prepares people to draw near.

---

[8] Reich, R (2013) *Jewish ritual baths in Judaea-Palaestina,* Yad Ben-Zvi and Israel Exploration Society, Jerusalem

The mikvah was never about hygiene; it was about holiness. (Leviticus 11:44; Leviticus 20:7–8). It stood as a witness in stone and water that God meets His people where cleansing and calling intersect. When a worshiper stepped into that pool, the issue was not ordinary dirt, but readiness to draw near. The immersion prepared the heart for presence. (Exodus 19:10–11; Psalm 24:3–4)

As David Webb observes, "God calls His people to consecration before construction. Before He builds through us, He washes us." (9) [9]

When a person descended those steps, the world narrowed. It was the moment between what had been and what was about to be.

Water That Waits for Covenant

The rhythm of the mikvah mirrored the rhythm of covenant life: separation before service, cleansing before calling.

Scripture does not speak of water in only one way. Priests were washed in consecration (Exodus 29:4). Priests also washed to approach and minister (Exodus 30:17–21). Israel knew purification washings for uncleanness and restoration (Leviticus 15:19–33; Numbers 19:19–21). Water already belonged to consecration, approach, and purification long before John stood in the Jordan.

---

[9] David Webb (2025) *Building the Kingdom Through the Local Church*, EKI Publishing

Gentiles entering Israel's covenant stepped into the mikvah to declare a new identity - *the old has passed away, behold, the covenant has begun.* (7,8,10–12) [10] [11] [12] [13] [14]

Hebrews later speaks of the doctrine of baptisms in the plural (Hebrews 6:1–2). Scripture itself refuses to flatten water into one thin idea. Consecration, approach, purification, and covenant transition already formed a broader water grammar long before the church ever filled a baptistry.

Covenants have always carried water somewhere in their story. (Genesis 6–9; Exodus 24:4–8; Numbers 19; Ezekiel 36:25–27) Before there was baptism, there was circumcision - a covenant mark cut into the flesh of Abraham's sons. It did not cleanse the conscience or forgive sin; it marked belonging. Circumcision marked the covenant in blood, but washing prepared the people who lived under the covenant.

But even then, Scripture hinted that flesh was never the final target. God spoke of hearts needing circumcision - of an inward alignment the knife could never reach. In Christ, the covenant moved from flesh to conscience. Paul explained it this way:

---

[10] *Mishnah Yevamot* 46a–47b;

[11] *Tosefta Kerithoth* 1:12;

[12] Josephus, *Antiquities* 13.257–258

[13] Reich, Ronny, (2013), *Miqwa'ot: Jewish Ritual Baths in the Second Temple Period and the Time of Jesus,* Jerusalem: Israel Exploration Society.

[14] Cohen, Shaye J.D. (1999), *The Beginnings of Jewishness,* University of California Press.

"You were circumcised with a circumcision made without hands, buried with Him in baptism." (Colossians 2:11–12)

The old covenant marked the body and regulated approach; the new reaches the conscience. (Hebrews 10:22; Titus 3:5; Acts 22:16) Circumcision marked belonging in flesh and blood; baptism speaks in the language of burial, cleansing, and identification by faith. (Galatians 3:26–27; Colossians 2:11–12) One cuts the flesh; the other cuts the old nature. One worked in shadow; the other gathers the shadow toward substance.

When you stand in the water, you are not negotiating a covenant – you are stepping into one already established. You are not purchasing a ticket into heaven, and you are not bargaining for favor. The covenant was sealed elsewhere - in blood. The covenant was sealed in Christ's blood; the water bears witness that you have entered it. Scripture speaks of *"three that bear witness on earth: the Spirit, and the water, and the blood"* (1 John 5:8). The blood secures the covenant, the Spirit gives life, and the water bears witness to what heaven has established.

The mikvah's water could not remove sin; it prepared hearts for the day when water would stand joined to the blood of the Lamb and the Name of Jesus in a fuller witness than cleansing dust ever could (Hebrews 9:13–14; Acts 2:38; Acts 22:16). It was rehearsal – preparation without finality.

The Quiet Preparation Before Glory

Before every divine movement, there was always a washing. Before the priest entered the tabernacle, he washed (Leviticus 16:4). Before Moses approached the mountain, the people washed their garments (Exodus 19:10–11). Before Jesus began His ministry, He stepped into the Jordan (Matthew 3:13–17).

The pattern never changed: God kept placing washing at the threshold of approach, service, and unveiling. Water did not force favor; it marked readiness for what God was about to do.

I learned something about that kind of preparation once, back in my early twenties. I was visiting a church where a friend from Bible college served as assistant pastor, and his grandfather was the pastor. I had known both men for years.

That Sunday morning, the church was full. I parked along the edge of the road and walked across the lot, not realizing that I had stepped in a patch of mud. By the time I reached the platform, the pastor - my friend's grandfather - looked down and said quietly, "Go wash your shoe off."

I asked, "Why?"

He said, "You've got mud on it."

I grew up in small country churches. Mud on your shoes was almost a badge of honor. But this congregation was different - a city church, full of well-dressed people, pressed suits, polished shoes, and soft voices. At first, I was a little offended. It seemed such a small thing to correct.

But I went.

I found the restroom, took off my shoe, and wiped the mud away. When I returned and the service began, I looked across that congregation and understood. In that setting, that tiny patch of dirt would have stood out to everyone. What I thought was insignificant could have distracted from everything else God wanted to do.

Standing there, I remembered Naaman - the man who almost missed his miracle because he didn't like the river God chose (2 Kings 5:10–14).

Sometimes the Lord isn't cleansing us because we're filthy; He's preparing us because we are approaching. (John 15:2; 2 Timothy 2:21). He's setting us apart because we're visible. The water before the work.

As Webb wrote, "The strength of the Church is not in its talent but in its purity; not in how loud we shout, but in how well we've been washed." (9) [15]

That is one reason the priestly washings matter. Scripture distinguishes between consecration and approach. Aaron and his sons were washed in consecration, but afterward they washed their

---

[15] Webb, David. (2025) *Building the Kingdom through the Local Church.* EKI Publishing.

hands and feet when drawing near to minister. Not every washing meant the same thing, and that matters when we come to baptism

Jesus later preserved that distinction with startling simplicity: *"He who has bathed needs only to wash his feet"* (John 13:10). Scripture itself knows the difference between a greater washing and the repeated cleansing needed in the walk. Not every recurring cleansing image points back to a fresh immersion.

The Mikvah and the Language of Readiness

The mikvah was not random. It taught Israel to think in the language of readiness, approach, and cleansing. Faithful Jews immersed before festivals, before prayer, before appointed moments of drawing near. Each washing said, not *"I am earning standing,"* but *"I am coming near in the way God appointed."*

That's why the mikvah sits at the intersection of humility and hope. God doesn't require spotless people; He calls *responsive* ones.

The water does not stand as humiliation, but as a witness that the approach to God is never casual.

When you step into the water, you are not proving yourself to God or earning a place before Him. You are answering His order of approach, saying, *"I'm ready for what You're ready to do."*

That is why John's baptism struck Israel with such force. John did not invent water. He summoned a nation back into its own water-language - repentance, readiness, and preparation for the One who was coming. His baptism did not stand as just another routine washing, and it did not yet exhaust what baptism would become in Christ. It stood at the threshold.

Reflection from the Water

The mikvah was more than a pool; it was a pause. A breath held between creation and covenant, calling and completion, shadow and substance. Every ripple whispered readiness. Every drop carried expectation.

When the kairos moment arrived, the mikvah stepped toward its Messianic purpose in a river called Jordan. The long rehearsal of Scripture was about to bear witness again.

Humanity had built altars beside rivers, but one day a river became the place where preparation, prophecy, and revelation met. The Jordan, already heavy with crossings, kings, and memory, was about to hear the Voice of creation speak again (Joshua 3:15–17; 2 Kings 5:10–14; Matthew 3:13–17) The same Voice that once hovered over the face of the waters was about to speak again - through a voice crying in the wilderness, the prophet who called a nation back to the water, preparing the way of the Lord.

Before there was baptism in the name of Jesus, there were people learning to meet God in water. (Exodus 29:4; Leviticus 15; Numbers 19; 2 Kings 5) They stepped down into stone pools, one after another, generation after generation - each washing a rehearsal for the day redemption would arrive.

Generation after generation stepped into the shadow, but the water was waiting for substance. And when that day finally came - when the Word (logos) made flesh stepped into the Jordan - the witnesses of creation appeared again: the Spirit moving, the water bearing, and the Voice declaring divine favor. (Genesis 1:2; Matthew 3:16) What the mikvah rehearsed in stillness, the river fulfilled in motion.

Scripture's water world had always been larger than a single rite or a single purpose. Consecration. Approach. Purification. Preparation. By the time Jesus stepped into the Jordan, the story was not beginning from nothing; it was gathering itself toward Him.

Scripture Index

- Colossians 2:11–12
- Exodus 19:10–11
- Exodus 29:4
- Ezekiel 36:25
- Galatians 3:26–27
- Genesis 1:2
- Hebrews 10:22
- Isaiah 40:3
- John 1:23
- John 15:2
- Joshua 3:15–17
- Leviticus 11:44
- Leviticus 12:1–8
- Leviticus 15:19–33
- Leviticus 16:4
- Matthew 3:13–17
- Numbers 19:19–21
- Psalm 24:3–4
- Titus 3:5
- 2 Kings 5:10–14
- 2 Timothy 2:21
- Exodus 30:17-21

- Hebrews 6:1-2
- John 13:10
- 1 John 5:8

- Acts 2:38
- Acts 22:16

Chapter Three

The River That Remembers

Long before the Jordan flowed beneath Israel's feet, rivers had already carried the prayers of humanity. Before Moses lifted his staff, the Nile had already carried him in the reeds. Before Joshua crossed into promise, humanity had already learned to meet water with hope in its heart and fear in its eyes. (Genesis 2:10–14). The river has always mirrored the human soul – restless, searching, and never still for long.

In Egypt, the Nile was more than a river; it was a god - the bloodline of a civilization. Priests washed in its flow before entering temples, believing the water would carry away impurity and awaken divine favor. (13) [16] In Mesopotamia, kings descended into the Euphrates as a sign of renewal, washing their bodies, weapons, and crowns – as though cleansing the tools of power could cleanse the heart that wielded them. (14) [17] In India, pilgrims still journey to the Ganges seeking release from stain. In Greece, lustration bowls stood at the entrance of every temple. Across

---

[16] Allen, James P.(2005) *The Ancient Egyptian Pyramid Texts. Atlanta:* SBL Press.
[17] Kramer, Samuel Noah.(1981) *History Begins at Sumer.* University of Pennsylvania Press.

cultures, water marked a threshold where the mortal reached
toward the immortal. (15) [18]

Every culture understood this much: to begin again, one
must first touch the water. The difference was never the washing –
it was in the *why*.

The Memory of the Waters

Water is one of the oldest witnesses on earth.(Genesis 1:2;
2 Peter 3:5–6) It carries memory (Psalm 77:16). It has been present
at every beginning. [19]

It remembers Eden's rivers, still tracing their courses
beneath the crust of history. It remembers the tears of slaves and
the laughter of kings. It has felt the blood of battle, the incense of
sacrifice, the songs of temples long buried beneath dust. It has
washed idols and prophets, pilgrims and corpses.

The water has seen it all.

Scripture is not embarrassed to speak this way. The earth
groans. The seas obey. The rocks are said to cry out. Heaven and
earth are called as witnesses. Blood speaks from the ground. Water
bears witness not because it is divine, but because creation answers
its Maker and can be appointed to testify to His acts.

And through centuries of ritual, one question lingered
beneath the surface: *Can water itself make a person clean?* The ancients

---

[18] Eliade, Mircea. (1959) *The Sacred and the Profane.* Harcourt, Ch. 2 "Water
and Regeneration."
[19] See Appendix B – Water Rembers

tried to wash away with rivers what only the blood of a better sacrifice could remove (Hebrews 10:1–4).

Then came a people whose God didn't live *in* the river - He moved *upon* it. (Genesis 1:2) Their story began not with superstition but with revelation. Their water wasn't divine; it was obedient. The difference between ritual and revelation is the difference between religion and relationship - one tries to climb to God; the other responds when He draws near. (1 Samuel 15:22; Isaiah 1:11–17; Micah 6:6–8)

The Counterfeit Waters

I was reminded of this while reading John Lawrence Reynolds' work on secret societies. (16) [20] What struck me was not the secrecy - it was the rituals.

Behind closed doors, these organizations practiced ceremonies that resembled baptism: initiations by water, vows sealed in shadow, oaths sworn beneath symbols of power. The parallels were unsettling. The rites promised enlightenment, access to hidden knowledge, and entry into a "chosen circle."

Many of these rites predate even the earliest Jewish writings. Across cultures and centuries, humanity carried a fractured memory of water as the doorway to transformation.

---

[20] Reynolds, John Lawrence (2006). *Secret Societies.* Key Porter Books Limited, Toronto. Canada.

But what startled me most was the *inversion*. What God had created as an open covenant was twisted into secret control. What once declared, *"I am washed and free,"* became an oath that whispered, *"I am bound and hidden."*

The adversary creates nothing of his own; he only corrupts what God has already called good. (Genesis 1:31; John 8:44; 2 Corinthians 11:14; Revelation 13:14) The water still remembers its purpose – even when those who step into it do not.

That is one reason baptism cannot be reduced to secrecy, private elitism, or hidden knowledge. God's water was never meant to disappear behind locked doors. It was meant to stand in the open as witness, not for public spectacle but for earnest obedience.

The River and the Word

In the beginning, the Word (logos) [21] spoke to the waters (Genesis 1:2–3; John 1:1–3). In every generation since, the water has been waiting to hear that Voice again.

The Egyptian priest chanted to the Nile, but the Nile never answered. Pharaoh's magicians could mimic signs, but they could not restore the river to its life-giving purpose. (Exodus 7:22; Exodus 8:7; Exodus 8:18) Kings knelt, philosophers washed, rituals repeated - but the soul remained unchanged.

---

[21] **"Word" note:** English *word* may translate **logos** (λόγος) or **rhēma** (ῥῆμα); in this book, when it matters, I bracket the term - (logos) or (rhēma) - to show which Greek word is in view (e.g., John 1:1; Luke 1:38).

But when the Word (logos) Himself stepped into the Jordan, the river *recognized* Him. (Mark 1:10–11; Psalm 114:3–7) It remembered the breath that once hovered upon its ancient surface. It remembered the Voice. What water had not yet seen - but was now being prepared for - was the blood of that same Word (logos) made flesh, the blood that would give its witness covenant weight (John 1:14; Hebrews 12:24).

The Jordan was not acting as a god. It was standing again where creation had always stood when God was revealing, dividing, cleansing, or beginning. Water remembers as witness remembers, by having stood where the Lord repeatedly acted.

Baptism, then, is not humanity reaching upward. It is God bending downward. When Jesus entered the Jordan, He was not inventing a new ritual; He was reclaiming an ancient witness. (1 Peter 3:20–21; Hebrews 10:22; Colossians 2:11–12).

He was also not stepping into a mere public display. He was gathering into Himself a water-language Scripture had been speaking for ages - creation, crossing, consecration, approach, cleansing, burial, and beginning - and standing in it as its fulfillment.

The Difference Between Ritual and Revelation

Pagans washed to appease gods. Israel washed to align with the One who had already spoken. Water can cleanse or drown, heal or destroy. What makes it holy is the Presence that moves upon it.

And yet even Presence does not bypass the cross. The Spirit moves upon the water, but it is the blood that gives the water its covenantal authority to witness to remission. Without the blood, the river can rinse the skin, but it cannot relieve the conscience (Hebrews 9:14).

That is why baptism cannot be treated as a ticket to heaven, a self-contained ritual act, or a religious photo opportunity. Water does not purchase what blood alone secured. But neither is baptism emptied into a hollow symbol. It stands where God appointed witness, approach, and response to meet obedience.

Reflection from the Deep

Perhaps that is why every culture has known how to wash – because something in us remembers Eden's rivers.

Humanity may have forgotten the sound of His voice, but the water never did.

And even now, when a soul steps into baptism, the river remembers. It listens again for the Voice, ready to bear witness to another beginning.

Not because water has life in itself, but because God has never treated it as meaningless. He appointed it to stand in too many beginnings, too many crossings, too many cleansings, and too many covenants for us to call it mere scenery now.

Scripture Index

- Genesis 2:10–14
- Psalm 77:16
- Genesis 1:2
- Genesis 1:2–3
- John 1:1–3
- 1 Samuel 15:22
- Genesis 1:31
- John 8:44
- Exodus 7:22
- Exodus 8:18
- Mark 1:10–11
- 1 Peter 3:21
- Isaiah 40:3
- Matthew 3:3
- Isaiah 1:11-17
- Micah 6:6-8
- 2 Corinthians 11:14
- Revelation 13:14
- Exodus 8:7
- Psalm 114:3-7
- John 1:14
- Hebrews 12:24
- Hebrews 10:22
- Colossians 2:11-12
- Hebrews 9:14
- 2 Peter 3:5-6

Chapter Four

The Wild Prophet and His River

Here Is Water

I once stood with a group of believers on a downtown riverfront, ministering to the homeless and the hungry. The city noise was our background choir - sirens, laughter, and passing traffic - but the Word (logos) of God cut through it all. People gathered, not because we were eloquent, but because they were thirsty.

As we prayed and shared the Gospel, I remembered the Ethiopian eunuch who, after hearing the words of Philip, said, *"See, here is water; what doth hinder me to be baptized?"* (Acts 8:36).

The river was right there - brown, shallow, and muddy. We looked at each other, took off our shoes, rolled up our pant legs, and walked down the boat ramp into the water. There was no choir, no robes, no marble font. Just ordinary people meeting God in ordinary water.

It reminded me that the power was never in polished surroundings and ceremony. It was in the moment where faith met the water that God had placed within reach of obedience. That moment on the riverfront felt like the Jordan all over again - not because of geography, but because of divine purpose. The same God who met people in the river had not lost His way there.

The Wettest Prophet in History

No prophet ever stayed wetter than John. He didn't thunder from marble steps or velvet pulpits; he shouted waist-deep in a muddy river. His robe was camel hair, his belt leather, his diet questionable - locusts drizzled with wild honey. He looked like a man who had lost an argument with the desert and decided to make it home anyway.

People came from everywhere to see him: priests from Jerusalem, shepherds from Judea, soldiers on leave, tax collectors clutching their conscience. (Matthew 3:5–6) They came because his words carried weight - because something ancient moved when he spoke. He was the kind of preacher who could make a Pharisee sweat and a sinner hope in the same sentence.

John's ministry wasn't polished - it was prophetic. He was the wettest prophet in history, and every sermon ended with a splash.

But John was not simply repeating the old washings. He stood at the threshold. His baptism belonged to repentance, readiness, and preparation for the One who was coming after him. He was not the finish. He was the voice before the unveiling.

The Prophet Who Wouldn't Fit In

If John walked into most churches today, security might escort him out before the first altar call. He smelled like wilderness, preached without filters, and refused to take offerings. But God used him precisely because he didn't fit.

Sometimes, favor dresses in camel hair. Sometimes the next move of God doesn't look respectable - it looks raw, untamed, inconvenient.

John's ministry was messy because repentance is messy. The Jordan wasn't chlorinated; it was brown with silt and stories. Each ripple carried confession, tears, laughter, and hope. It wasn't elegant - but it was effective.

That is what made John's ministry so unsettling. He was not a bitter outsider shouting at a world he had never touched. Priesthood ran in his blood (Luke 1:5). He had every natural reason to serve within the recognized order of his day, yet the word of God drove him to the Jordan instead. The priestly son stood outside the sanctioned spaces, summoning even the religious establishment to repent. God was not abandoning holiness; He was confronting hypocrisy and making room for repentance in a place the gatekeepers did not own.

The River of Repentance

Repentance isn't punishment; it's permission. It's the moment heaven says, *"Turn around - I'm behind you."* John's ministry revealed that God's favor wasn't waiting in temples but rising in rivers.

As David Webb writes, repentance is not shame - it is alignment. It is the Father inviting His people back into readiness, washing the heart before He releases the assignment. (9) [22]

Repentance clears the ground. It breaks agreement with what distorted us and makes room for what God is restoring within.(3) [23]

The wilderness crowd was learning something the priests had forgotten: you do not have to be polished or perfect to prepare; you only have to be willing to turn and come near in the way God appoints. That is why John's baptism carried such force. It was not a temple washing repeated out of habit. It was a prophetic summons in water - a call for Israel to turn, prepare, and stand ready for the Messiah.

When the Messiah finally came to that same river, John trembled. He saw in Jesus the fulfillment of every wave, every echo, every baptism that had come before. And in that trembling voice, the old world met the new.

John knew the difference between his water and Christ's fullness. He could summon people to repentance, but he could not be the One to fulfill what the river had been waiting for. His baptism pointed forward. Christ gathered the witness into Himself.

---

[22] Webb, David (2025). *Building the Kingdom Through the Local Church*, EKI Publishing.
[23] Rice, Kevin (2023). *Cultivating the New Nature*. EKI Publishing

Chapter Five

The Priest in the Water

A River for the Restless

The Jordan was his pulpit; the wilderness his choir. When John cried, *"Repent, for the kingdom of heaven is at hand!"* (Matthew 3:2), it wasn't condemnation - it was invitation. He wasn't wagging a finger; he was opening a door.

John did not call people into a managed religious space. He called them out to the Jordan. Men were used to water near the holy places of Jerusalem, but John's river stood outside the reach of priestly control and official approval. That was part of the shock. The prophet was summoning a nation to prepare for God in a place no religious system could fully manage.

Repentance meant turning - not simply feeling bad or guilty, but changing direction before the arrival of the King. John's baptism was *unto repentance* (Mark 1:4; Luke 3:3): a turning before the Lord Himself appeared. The people waded in not to earn forgiveness but to admit their direction was wrong. Behind that turning was something deeper than fear - it was godly sorrow, the kind Paul later described as producing repentance that leads to somewhere real *"produces repentance leading to salvation (sōtēria - inheritance-outcome)."* [24] (2 Corinthians 7:10) - a sorrow that does not

---

[24] See Appendix H - Sōzō Soteria: Rescue, Formation, and Inheritance

end in regret, but moves toward God's intended outcome. The same Father who would later draw Nicodemus by night was already drawing Israel to the riverbank.

Every plunge beneath the water said, *"I can't keep walking this way."* Every rise from the current whispered, *"Make ready the path of the Lord."* (Isaiah 40:3) Their tears were real, their turning sincere. But John's river could only prepare them. The Lamb's blood had not yet been poured out, and without that blood there could be no full new-covenant remission – only anticipation (Hebrews 9:22).

They didn't know yet that the path would soon walk toward them.

The Wilderness Voice

The wilderness had waited a long time for a prophet. (Psalm 74:9; Amos 8:11) For four centuries, heaven had been silent - no visions, no angels, no new word from God. Then a cry broke the stillness. Not from a palace or a temple but from a ravine along the Jordan.

John did not come to the Jordan as a religious outsider with no rightful claim to holy things. He came as a son of priestly blood. His father had served at the altar, his household stood in Aaron's line, and he would have understood the rhythms of temple order from childhood. John was no low servant on the margins by lineage; he was an Aaronic son called into a higher obedience than institutional location could contain. Yet God did not station him behind the courts of managed religion. He sent him to the river. The priest was called outside the structure - not because holiness had diminished, but because obedience had widened. John's ministry was proof that God could take a man with every natural credential for the system and send him beyond it when the hour demanded a holier kind of readiness.

John's sermons were short and sharp, like stones flung by a shepherd: *"Prepare. Repent. The ax is at the root."* (Luke 3:9; Matthew 3:10) *"Bear fruit worthy of repentance."* (Matthew 3:8) *"Don't claim lineage; live transformation."* (Luke 3:8; Matthew 3:9)

He was fire wrapped in flesh - the echo of Elijah reborn in rough skin and holy defiance (Malachi 4:5–6; Matthew 11:14). He had no interest in titles - only testimonies. The wilderness had finally found its voice again, and even the stones seemed to listen.

John did not stand there merely to revive an old custom. He stood there to gather all the old water-language into one prophetic summons: Israel, turn. The King is near. Come to the river prepare to meet Him.

Between the Old and the New

John stood at history's hinge - one foot in prophecy, one foot in promise. He was the final link in a long chain of preparation: priests, prophets, mikvah keepers, dreamers who washed before they worshiped. He gathered their symbols into one loud declaration: *"The King is coming. Get in the water."*

His baptism was not yet baptism into the risen Christ; it was preparatory water at the threshold - a call to repentance, readiness, and conscience-awakening before the Messiah was revealed more fully. (Acts 19:1–5) It looked backward to Israel's rivers of repentance and forward to the day when the Lamb of God would gather the witness into Himself.

When people asked, *"Are you the Messiah?"* he answered plainly, *"No. I baptize you with water; but one is coming who will baptize you with the Holy Spirit and with fire."* (Luke 3:16; Matthew 3:11; Mark 1:7–8) He knew his place: the forerunner, not the finish line.

John's water mattered, but John knew its limit. His baptism could turn a people, but it could not become the thing toward which it pointed. He was the voice before the unveiling, not the unveiling itself.

The Priest in The Water

John wasn't just a prophet - he was a priest. Before he ever cried in the wilderness, priesthood ran in his blood. He was the son of Zechariah, a priest of the division of Abijah (Luke 1:5), a son of Aaron, a descendant of Levi (Numbers 18:1–7).

Every time John lowered someone into the Jordan, he was knowingly stepping into an ancient assignment. The sons of Aaron had been washed before service (Exodus 29:4; Leviticus 8:6), and priests later washed again when drawing near to minister. John stood in that world, but his river gave it prophetic force. What John handled in priestly shadow would soon be opened in Christ to a people made *"a royal priesthood"* (1 Peter 2:9). He stood in his priestly position, receiving and examining those who presented themselves to be sanctified and set apart.

This was no casual wade into religious sentiment. In Israel, men did not draw near to holy service by impulse alone. Priests were washed before ministry (Exodus 29:4; Leviticus 8:6), washed again when approaching sacred duty (Exodus 30:19–21), and in higher moments of consecration bathed their flesh before putting on holy garments (Leviticus 16:4). The law did not treat purification as decorative. It treated it as readiness. There were even moments in Israel's history when the priests themselves failed in this duty, and the Levites had to step in because they had been more diligent to sanctify themselves (2 Chronicles 29:34; 30:3, 15–17). Title was not enough. Proximity was not enough. Holy things required preparation.

So when John stood in the Jordan, he was not acting like a desert eccentric telling people to go skinny-dip before church. He stood there as a priest in prophetic office, receiving those who came confessing, turning, and presenting themselves for sanctification. He was not inventing the water-language of Israel; he was gathering it, inspecting those who entered it, and pressing an old priestly demand into a new prophetic hour: if you would meet the coming King, you do not stroll into His presence unchanged. You turn. You submit. You come washed and made ready.

But something happened the day Jesus appeared on the riverbank.

A priest stood in the water… and the Great High Priest stepped toward him. For we have a *"great High Priest who has passed through the heavens - Jesus the Son of God"* (Hebrews 4:14), the One declared *"a priest forever after the order of Melchizedek"* (Hebrews 5:6).

The shadow reached for the substance. The old order laid hands on the new. Levi touched Melchizedek.

When John baptized Jesus, the priest washed the Lamb (John 1:29). He who knew no sin stepped into the waters that had carried every repentant cry before Him.

It was more than repentance. More than preparation. It was priestly witness meeting priestly fulfillment. It was the priesthood passing the torch.

And from that moment forward, everyone baptized into Christ would share in His priesthood - for He made us "a royal priesthood, a holy nation" (1 Peter 2:9). Not in rank, but in representation, not in Levitical ritual, but in resurrection authority.

This is why baptism in the name of Jesus could move beyond Levitical hands without losing holy weight: the priestly stream had been opened wider than Levi (Matthew 28:19), because they were standing in the priestly stream Jesus opened.

When a believer baptizes another, they are not performing a ceremony; they are participating in a priesthood. They are acting under the authority of the One who was washed, affirmed, and declared beloved in the Jordan's flowing aisle (Matthew 3:16–17).

The river that once washed priests now washes priests again - sons and daughters of the Great High Priest, joining His ministry one baptism at a time.

And that is why baptism cannot be reduced to a church ritual, a public performance, or a ticket-to-heaven formula. Priestly waters never belonged to spectacle. They belonged to approach, consecration, and witness before God.

Reflection from the River

John was the bridge between silence and song. His sermons were sandpaper for the soul. His river was the rehearsal for redemption.

Alignment always precedes release. John's obedience did not create the move of God - he stood where he was told to stand, and there the river became a threshold. (17) [25]

He stood dripping with purpose, shouting what prophets had whispered for centuries: *Make ready the way of the Lord!*

The day John announced had arrived. The One he had cried about now stood in the current, and creation seemed to hold its breath (Matthew 3:16–17; Mark 1:10–11). The river that had

---

[25] Rite, KM (2025) *Unchained: Freed to be His Treasure*. EKI Publishing.

flowed since Genesis carried its oldest memory again - not as shadow or rehearsal, but as Presence (Genesis 1:2). What the water witnessed in preparation, it was now witnessing in fulfillment.

John had spent his life calling people into the water. Then one day the reason for the river stepped into it.

Scripture Index

- Acts 19:1–5
- Amos 8:11
- Genesis 1:2
- Isaiah 40:3
- Luke 3:3
- Luke 3:8
- Luke 3:9
- Luke 3:16
- Malachi 4:5–6
- Mark 1:4
- Mark 1:7–8
- Mark 1:10–11
- Matthew 3:2
- Matthew 3:8
- Matthew 3:9
- Matthew 3:10
- Matthew 3:11
- Matthew 3:16–17
- Matthew 11:14
- Psalm 74:9
- Numbers 18:1–7
- Luke 1:5
- Hebrews 4:14
- Hebrews 5:6
- 1 Peter 2:9
- Hebrews 9:22
- Exodus 29:4
- Exodus 30:17-21
- Leviticus 8:6
- John 1:29

Part Two: Making Waves

Jesus and the Waters of Fulfillment

When the Son of God enters the water, every earlier witness begins to gather around Him. He did not come to be cleansed, but to stand in the river where preparation gives way to fulfillment.

Chapter Six

The Day Jesus Got Dunked

That day in the Jordan, He wasn't simply washed - He was rehearsing resurrection. Every movement in that water held a shadow of what would come three years later. (Luke 12:50) When Jesus stepped into the Jordan, He wasn't repenting of sin - He was revealing a pattern. His baptism was more than obedience; it was prophecy in motion. The moment His body sank beneath the surface, a shadow of the cross rippled across the river. The water received the Son of God like a grave receives the dead - not to keep Him, but to witness what only heaven could release.

But resurrection was only one layer; His baptism also stood in the long water-language of priestly consecration and preparation for ministry.

Before a priest could lift a hand in the service of God, he first passed through water. The sons of Levi washed before entering the tent of meeting (Exodus 29:4; Leviticus 8:6). They did not minister until they had been washed, confirmed, and appointed for service at the age of thirty (Numbers 4:3, Numbers 30). When Jesus, the true and final High Priest, came to the Jordan at about thirty years of age (Luke 3:23), the timing itself stood inside that priestly shadow. He was not repenting of sin but fulfilling every shadow that pointed to Him. John - the son of a priest, a descendant of Aaron (Luke 1:5) - stood waist-deep in that ancient current, ministering in the same broad water-world where priests had long been washed for service and had later washed again to draw near (Exodus 30:17–21). The river was no basin, but the stream of preparation had reached its appointed hour.

Yet this was no ordinary priesthood. He was not of Levi's order but of a higher covenant - *"a priest forever after the order of Melchizedek"* (Hebrews 5:6; Psalm 110:4).

And if He stepped into the water as Priest, He also stepped into it as the Lamb that the priest would identify and present. In the old covenant, every sacrifice had to be inspected and washed by the hands of a priest before it could be offered (Exodus 12:3–6; Leviticus 22:17–20; Leviticus 1:3–9). The priest identified the offering, declared its purpose, and presented it before the Lord - a role recorded not only in Scripture but reflected in early Jewish practice. (7,11) [26] When John lifted his voice on the riverbank and cried, *"Behold, the Lamb of God who takes away the sin of the world!"* (John 1:29), he was not giving Jesus a poetic title. He was performing a priestly act:

- identifying the Lamb,

---

[26] **Priestly Inspection & Declaration in Second Temple Judaism:**
The Mishnah records that priests were required to **state the intention** of a sacrifice and declare its acceptability (Mishnah *Zevachim* 2:1–2). Lambs were inspected for blemish and verbally designated for their purpose (*Pesachim* 5:5–7). Josephus, a first-century priest, writes that priests "examined the sacrifices to ensure they were without blemish, and declared them fit for offering" (*Antiquities* 3.224–225). These practices reflect a consistent pattern of priestly *identification* and *designation* that parallels John's declaration in John 1:29.

- declaring the purpose of the sacrifice,

- and presenting Him before God and Israel.

John, a priest by lineage and prophet by calling, became the final Levitical priest to inspect the final Lamb. The Jordan became the laver and threshold before the altar - the place where the purity of the Lamb was revealed, and His ministry consecrated. The heavens opened. The Spirit descended like a dove (Matthew 3:16; Isaiah 42:1; Psalm 2:7). The Father's voice echoed through the Jordan valley, *"This is My beloved Son, in whom I am well pleased."* (Matthew 3:17) What once required ritual now bowed before reality. Priesthood, kingship, and sacrifice converged in that one moment, finding their fulfillment in the body of the Lamb.

In that single scene, heaven took record[27] and earth bore witness: just as in the beginning, when the voice of God spoke over the waters and creation responded. The Father speaking from above, the Son (logos) standing in the water, and the Spirit descending. And on earth the witnesses gathered as well, the Spirit resting upon Him, the water receiving Him, and within Him the blood that would soon be poured out - the very three that would one day be named together as bearing *"witness on earth"* (1 John 5:8).

---

[27] Scripture consistently presents heaven as the place of record and judgment rather than witness (cf. Malachi 3:16; Daniel 7:10; Psalm 56:8; Revelation 20:12).

David Webb describes this convergence as "the moment Heaven's order touched earth's altar." (9) [28]

All of it - priesthood, sacrifice, washing, anointing, and declaration - was moving toward one revelation: the death, burial, and resurrection He would soon embody. Paul later described believers as being *"buried with Him in baptism"* (Romans 6:3–4). The river had already preached that motion in shadow: down - burial, under - surrender, up - new breath.

When you step into the water, you are not purchasing heaven, and you are not acting out a hollow ceremony. You are stepping into a witness shaped by death, burial, and resurrection. Every immersion is a living sermon preached by motion - an act that says, *"I have been crucified with Christ; nevertheless, I live."* (Galatians 2:20). The old nature does not leave quietly; it is buried. That is why baptism speaks with such force. (3) [29]

The Jordan became His stage - but also His rehearsal. Because what He enacted in the water that day, He fulfilled in the tomb three years later. He was baptized into death before He was buried in stone (Romans 6:3–4; Colossians 2:12), so that when He rose again, the river already knew His name. And if the river knew Him, it knew Him as witness knows - by having stood where God appointed death, consecration, priesthood, sacrifice, anointing, and declaration to meet in one body. And so, because His baptism

---

[28] Webb, David (2025). *Building the Kingdom Through the Local Church*. EKI Publishing.
[29] Rice, Kevin (2023) *Cultivating the New Nature*, EKI Publishing

rehearsed our resurrection, every time we enter the water the pattern speaks again: death to the old self, burial of what cannot follow, resurrection into a life that breathes differently. Baptism isn't about escaping life; it is entry into life as one who has passed through death with Christ and now lives resurrected to the true nature God designed in us from the beginning.

All throughout the Old Testament, the water kept whispering a story in shadows. Priests washed before their service, lambs were washed before their sacrifice, Israel washed before their worship. The Red Sea carried a nation from slavery, and the Jordan carried them into promise. These were not empty rituals; they were rehearsals - shadows of a substance waiting for its moment (Hebrews 10:1).

When Jesus stepped into the Jordan, the shadows did not disappear as though they had meant nothing. They gathered into the Light that revealed what they had been pointing toward all along. What the priests acted, what the lambs pictured, what the crossings foretold - He fulfilled (Colossians 2:17).

And now, in our baptism, we do not return to the shadow or the rehearsal. As He was washed and presented as the Lamb, so we are washed and presented in Him - as living sacrifices, participating in what He fulfilled. We step into the substance Himself - the death, burial, and resurrection we share with Christ (Romans 6:3–4). The water no longer points forward; it points back to the Lamb who made it real.

That is why this water can never be reduced to a photo-op, a public confession cliché, or a denominational checkbox. Too much converged in the Jordan for baptism to be treated as a small religious gesture now.

Scripture Index

- Luke 12:50
- Exodus 29:4
- Leviticus 8:6
- Numbers 4:3
- Luke 3:23
- Luke 1:5
- Exodus 30:17–21
- Hebrews 5:6
- Psalm 110:4
- Exodus 12:3–6
- Leviticus 22:17–20
- Leviticus 1:3–9
- John 1:29
- Matthew 3:16
- Isaiah 42:1
- Psalm 2:7
- Matthew 3:17
- 1 John 5:8
- Galatians 2:20
- Romans 6:3–4
- Colossians 2:12
- Colossians 2:17
- Hebrews 10:1

Chapter Seven

When Repentance Met Righteousness

Two Men, One River, Two Purposes

John stood waist-deep in the Jordan, preaching his one-note sermon with thunder in his throat. *"Repent, for the kingdom of heaven is at hand!"* (Matthew 3:2) No choir. No fog machine. Just a prophet who looked like yesterday's wilderness and smelled like tomorrow's revival.

People stepped into the water like soldiers into surrender. Every immersion said, *"I can't keep walking this way."* John's baptism was unto repentance (Mark 1:4) - a physical act that marked a heart turning from rebellion toward readiness. It was a movement born of conviction, not performance.

Then Jesus appeared on the shoreline. The sinless among the sorry. The Creator among the created. And He got in line.

John came from the tribe of Levi -the sons of Aaron, born to wash and to warn. Jesus came from the tribe of Judah - the sons of David, born to rule and redeem. Yet, in the providence of God, these two streams met in the same bloodline. Mary and Elizabeth were kin, their wombs carrying the covenant's two halves: priesthood and kingship. In Jordan, those lines merged again. The priest met the King, the herald met the Heir, and the water stood witness. The river that once prepared priests now received the

Lord of priests. The hands that served at the altar now lowered the Lamb of God beneath the current. In that moment, Heaven saw what earth had long awaited - Levi and Judah, Law and Mercy, priesthood and kingship, family and fulfillment - all joined in one act of obedience.

Where Jesus stepped down before him, John blinked, half in awe, half in panic. *"I need to be baptized by You, and You come to me?"* (Matthew 3:14) That's prophet-speak for, *"You've got this backward, Lord."*

But Jesus answered, calm and steady: *"Allow it now, for thus it becomes us to fulfill all righteousness."* (Matthew 3:15)

John's baptism called a people to turn. Jesus' baptism stood in that same river for another purpose - fulfillment, alignment, and the public unveiling of the Son and the Lamb. One river held both movements that day: repentance rising from earth, righteousness descending from heaven.

John's baptism looked backward - to regret and repentance. Jesus' baptism looked forward - to fulfillment and alignment. Two baptisms, two directions, one river.

And almost immediately, Scripture shows what happens when heaven begins shifting the current. *"There arose a question… about purifying"* (John 3:25). That word matters. People weren't treating baptism like theatre; they were already linking water to cleansing, to transition, to what makes a person *clean* before God. John came from priestly stock (Luke 1:5), and Jesus was known as

Judah's Lion (Hebrews 7:14), so the question of "who baptizes" would not have felt small. But the question about purification quickly exposed something else: anxiety over authority and attention. John's disciples came and said, *"He… baptizeth, and all men come to him"* (John 3:26). In plain terms: *our river is losing its crowd.*

That moment is not there to shame John's followers; it's there to show how humans react when God moves the spotlight. John didn't defend his lane. He interpreted the shift: what he carried was given *"from heaven,"* and what Jesus carried was greater still (John 3:27–30). The river was never a platform. It was a witness. And the witness was pointing forward the whole time."

The Humility That Shocked Heaven

No spotlight. No choir robe. Just mud, water, and majesty stooping beneath a prophet's hand. Perfection submitted to purpose, and heaven couldn't stay silent.

It's funny - centuries earlier, a man named Naaman had stood on this same riverbank and refused to dip in the Jordan. He wanted a cleaner river, something ceremonial and respectable. (2 Kings 5:10–14) He didn't understand that holiness isn't about clarity; it's about obedience.

Jesus did what Naaman almost didn't - He stepped willingly into muddy water, because it wasn't about taking a bath. It was about fulfilling a purpose. The Jordan wasn't pure because of its color; it became holy because God appointed it for that moment. Jesus didn't wait for better conditions; He submitted to the Father's will within them.

That's the difference between religion and revelation: religion looks for clean water; revelation steps into whatever God has called holy.

When Jesus came up out of the water, the sky tore open. A dove descended. A Voice rolled across the valley: *"This is My beloved Son, in whom I am well pleased."* (Matthew 3:16–17)

Heaven wasn't reacting to spectacle; it was recognizing alignment. Jesus didn't need forgiveness; He embodied the Father's delight. He didn't cleanse Himself; His Presence consecrated the current. The river that had washed sinners now carried the smile of God.

When Repentance Meets Righteousness

That day, two tides met in one stream - repentance from below and favor from above (Isaiah 64:1; Mark 1:10–11). And in that moment, the four hundred years of silence shattered; heaven opened, and God spoke again to a waiting world. [30]

The Spirit had once hovered over the waters of creation (Genesis 1:2); now He rested upon the waters of redemption. Same Spirit. Same element. A new moment in the story.

---

[30] See Intertestamental Period: 1 Maccabees; Josephus, Antiquities 13–20 — documenting prophetic silence between Malachi and John.

From that moment, baptism could no longer be spoken of only as turning from what was behind. In Jesus, water now also bore witness to righteousness, sonship, favor, and the descent of the Spirit.

Repentance was not discarded in that river. It was joined by fulfillment. John brought a people to the water in readiness. Jesus stepped into the same current and filled it with a deeper witness.

No Stage, No Spotlight

Somewhere in church history, we turned baptism into a selfie for the saved [31] - a public confession, a moment for applause (Matthew 6:1). But Scripture never makes that connection. There isn't a single verse where baptism is commanded as a public performance.

Confession happens with the mouth (Romans 10:9–10). Baptism happens with the body. One speaks. The other surrenders.

Tradition made baptism a performance; heaven made it a witness. Somebody turned baptism into a stage announcement - but heaven never handed out microphones.

Older immersion instincts were far less curated than ours. Jewish teaching treated true immersion with a severity modern baptism culture would find uncomfortable, and the point ran

---

[31] See Appendix H - Sōzō and Soteria: Rescue, Formation, and Inheritance

deeper than ritual form. In the older purification world, washing and examination could stand together. The act was severe enough to expose what was there - blemish, uncleanness, reality. Nothing hidden. Nothing staged. Nothing between the person and the water. That does not mean the church should chase shock; it means we should stop pretending baptism was designed to preserve appearances. It was meant to bring a life into the light. We have dressed it up so thoroughly that we have nearly forgotten how direct it once was.

It was never meant to be a show, but a summons - an embodied obedience that heaven records whether anyone on earth applauds or not. Baptism isn't a formula for rescue; it's an invitation into alignment. And in that alignment, something holy happens: the Name meets the water (Acts 10:48), and what Ananias told Saul still echoes - *"Arise, and be baptized, and wash away your sins, calling on the name of the Lord."* (Acts 22:16)

The water doesn't cleanse by magic; it cleanses by meeting the mandate of His Name. Obedience opens what ceremony could never earn.

It's not about who's watching; it's about Who's waiting. Heaven isn't applauding a performance; it's authorizing a transformation.

The Joined Message

At Pentecost, Peter stood before the crowd and joined repentance and baptism in one apostolic command: *"Repent, and be baptized every one of you in the name of Jesus Christ for the remission of sins, and you shall receive the gift of the Holy Spirit."* (Acts 2:38)

John's river had preached repentance. Jesus' river revealed righteousness. Peter now preached remission and the gift of the Spirit, not by invention but by delegated authority (Matthew 28:19)- the outward witness met the inward gift.

Repentance turns. Righteousness aligns. Remission releases (Luke 24:47). Favor affirms. And the Spirit seals it all with Presence.

In Him, the washing of the priest, the anointing of the king, and the cleansing of the lamb all found completion. And now, we who follow are called not to repeat the shadow, but to enter the pattern as *living sacrifices*. (Romans 12:1). In Him we are washed, inspected, and presented before God without spot or blemish, and brought into our *"reasonable service."* The water that once prepared priests and lambs now stands witness for sons and daughters. What was shadow has opened into living participation.

Reflection from the River

Two baptisms met that day - repentance rising from the earth and righteousness descending from heaven. When they touched, the silence of four centuries shattered, and the river learned a new song.

And ever since, every believer steps somewhere in that same melody. Some come with regret, some with readiness, all with a longing to be aligned to Him. The water remembers His weight, His footprints, His obedience - and it waits for ours.

Because baptism is more than water over a body; it is a life stepping into His pattern: down in surrender, under in silence, up in newness of life. The Jordan opened the future for Him, and baptism opens the future for us - inviting every heart to walk in the favor, the alignment, the obedience, and the resurrection He revealed in that river.

The river did not become holy because men watched. It became holy because heaven spoke there. And baptism still carries its weight the same way.

Scripture Index

- Isaiah 64:1
- Luke 15:20–24
- Luke 12:50
- Mark 1:10–11
- Matthew 6:1
- Acts 10:48
- Genesis 1:2
- Hebrews 7:14
- John 3:25-30
- Luke 1:5
- Luke 24:47
- Mark 1:4
- Matthew 3:2
- Matthew 3:14-17
- Matthew 28:19
- Romans 10:9-10

- Romans 12:1
- 2 Kings 5:10-14
- Acts 2:38
- Acts 22:16

Chapter Eight

Born of Water and Spirit

The Night Visit

Nicodemus came to Jesus after dark - maybe to avoid the eyes of the crowd, maybe because deep questions need the quiet. He was a scholar, a leader, fluent in Torah and temple talk. But something about Jesus - the miracles, the mercy, the authority - shook his categories. He came with a question about miracles. Jesus answered with a revelation about birth.

"Rabbi, we know You are a teacher come from God; no one can do these miracles unless God is with him." (John 3:2)

Jesus didn't nod politely. He went straight to the root: *"Except a man be born again, he cannot see the kingdom of God."* (John 3:3)

Nicodemus blinked. Born again? From what? Into what? He wasn't confused because he was slow; he was confused because Jesus had shifted the conversation from behavior to birth.

What drew Nicodemus to Jesus that night wasn't curiosity alone; it was the Father's pull - the unseen persuasion Jesus later described when He said, *'No man can come to Me unless the Father who sent Me draws him'* (John 6:44). New birth doesn't begin with man climbing upward; it begins with God leaning downward.

Conception and Birth

Jesus wasn't describing moral reform; He was revealing a spiritual gestation.

"Born again" also means *born from above* - a conception begun in heaven, not in human effort. James wrote, *"By His own will He brought us forth through the word (logos) of truth"* (James 1:18). Peter echoed him: *"You have been born again… by the living and incorruptible seed of the Word (logos)"* (1 Peter 1:23).

That is conception - when the seed of the Word (logos) [32] meets faith in the heart. The new birth starts with a seed. God speaks, truth enters, and something eternal begins to form.

The Word (logos) does not merely inform - it impregnates. It is the heavenly record touching earthly soil, the seed of God finding agreement in the heart. Without the Word (logos), nothing is conceived; without water and Spirit, nothing is born.

But Jesus wasn't talking about conception alone. In Scripture, conception begins life, but birth releases it.

Anyone who has ever waited through a labor knows the moment - the water breaks, and suddenly what was hidden is pressing toward birth. The water did not create the life; it witnessed that the life was ready to come forth. Jesus' words to Nicodemus carry that same gravity. He is not speaking only of

---

[32] In this book, I use logos for the Word as God's declared truth, and rhema for that Word made living and present to the hearer. One is the seed spoken; the other is the seed awakened. For fuller definitions of logos and rhema, see Glossary of Terms.

something conceived in secret, but of something heaven means to bring forth into open life.

Something must break water before a child is born. Something must break water and Spirit before a believer enters the Kingdom. Born again begins the life. Born of water and Spirit brings it forth.

The Word (logos) gives life its beginning.

The water gives life its boundary.

The Spirit gives life its breath.

That is why Jesus does not speak loosely here. He is not tossing out religious poetry. He is describing how heaven begins what earth must eventually witness.

John would later describe new birth as the convergence of what God initiates above and what He confirms below. New life does not begin in human resolve but in divine action - when the Father draws, the Word (logos) gives seed, and the Spirit awakens the heart (John 1:12–13; James 1:18; 1 Peter 1:23). That is the unseen origin of life, conceived by God before it is ever expressed by man.

But what God initiates in heaven is never left without testimony on earth. The same Spirit who awakens the heart bears witness in the life begun. [33] The water marks obedience. [34] The blood secures remission. [35] Together, they confirm outwardly what

---

[33] See Appendix E - The Witness of the Spirit
[34] See Appendix B – The Witness of the Water
[35] See Appendix D – The Witness of the Blood

God has already begun inwardly (John 3:5; Romans 6:3–4; Hebrews 12:24).

Conception begins where God speaks life; birth is manifested where that life is surrendered, washed, and witnessed. What is conceived by the Word of God (*logos*) is awakened as that same Word becomes living and present to the hearer (*rhema*), [36] delivered through obedience, and confirmed by the witnesses God has appointed. New birth, then, is not a single moment but a divine agreement - heaven initiating, earth responding, and God testifying that a new life has truly begun.

Logos is the conceiving Word. Rhema is not a second seed, but the revealed Word breaking open what Logos conceived. One plants life; the other brings that life to the threshold of birth.

Two Births in One Conversation

Jesus didn't stop at "born again." He continued: *"Except a man be born of water and of the Spirit, he cannot enter the kingdom of God."* (John 3:5)

I have heard it said that the water Jesus spoke of was the water of a natural birth. But Jesus did not say, "You must be born again of your mother's water." He said, *"born of water and of the Spirit."* Nicodemus had dragged the conversation backward into

---

[36] In this book, I use logos for the Word as God's declared truth, and rhema for that Word made living and present to the hearer. One is the seed spoken; the other is the seed awakened. For fuller definitions of logos and rhema, see Glossary of Terms.

the womb; Jesus pulled it forward into the Kingdom. If "water" is reduced to natural birth, then consistency demands the same of "Spirit," for the word is *pneuma* - breath, wind, life-force. By that logic, Jesus would be saying, "You must be born of fluid and breath" - a poetic description of childbirth that every living man has already experienced. That is not revelation - it is redundancy. [37]

The Lord was not explaining how a baby enters the world; He was revealing how a believer enters the Kingdom: the water witnesses, the Spirit breathes, and what the Word conceived is finally brought to birth.

The first birth - born again - opens your eyes: you can see the Kingdom.

The second birth - born of water and Spirit - opens the door: you do not just glimpse the Kingdom; you can step into it and begin to live the restored life it offers.

The first is revelation (life conceived).

The second is regeneration (life delivered).

Many conceive truth; fewer carry it to birth.

Seeing is revelation. Entering is participation.

Plenty of people can recognize truth; fewer choose to walk through it. They've conceived life but never brought it forth.

---

[37] This interpretation appears to import a later childbirth idiom into an ancient conversation. Later English can use "water" for amniotic fluid - the Oxford English Dictionary's earliest cited English example is c. 1450 - but there is no clear ancient Jewish or Greco-Roman evidence that "born of water" functioned as a stock expression for natural birth in Nicodemus' world. D. A. Carson likewise notes that he has not found such usage in the ancient sources.

Many recognize the Kingdom; fewer enter it.

But even revelation cannot deliver what only redemption can secure. The heart can awaken to truth long before the blood speaks its better things (Hebrews 12:24). Nicodemus was beginning to see, but seeing is not cleansing - and cleansing requires a price.

That is the ache in this conversation. Nicodemus was not being invited merely to admire the Kingdom from a distance. He was being summoned to be born into it.

The Prophetic Blueprint

Jesus wasn't inventing new language that night; He was unveiling an ancient promise Nicodemus already knew by heart. Hidden in Ezekiel's scrolls was the blueprint of the new birth:

"I will sprinkle clean water upon you… I will give you a new heart… and I will put My Spirit within you." (Ezekiel 36:25–27)

Nicodemus had taught these words for years, but he had never stood in front of the One who embodied them. Water. Word. Spirit. Cleansing, reshaping, indwelling - not three separate stages, but three movements of a single miracle.

Ezekiel's vision aligned perfectly with what Jesus was now reveling: the Father draws, the Word (logos) begets, the water witnesses, the Spirit indwells. Heaven bears record; earth bears witness. What God initiates above finds expression below.

Most rabbis read Ezekiel as a prophecy of national renewal, but Jesus treated it as the architecture of spiritual birth. Ezekiel wasn't describing a linear sequence; he was describing a divine convergence. The Word (logos) would carve a new heart, soft where stone once lived, receptive to the voice of God. The water would cleanse, removing what could not follow into covenant. And the Spirit would breathe into that renewed heart, animating what the Word (logos) had conceived and the water had prepared.

This wasn't moral reform; it was new creation.

It wasn't improvement; it was birth.

Yet even this blueprint awaited one more element - the blood that would ratify the covenant it described. The Word (logos) plants life, the water unveils it, the Spirit animates it, but only the blood secures it. Without the blood, the water could cleanse the body, but not the conscience (Hebrews 9:13–14).

Nicodemus had studied these passages his entire life. But for the first time, the pieces aligned. The birth Jesus described was not a doctrine to master but a reality to enter. The very same elements that hovered over the waters of Genesis now hovered over Nicodemus' understanding.

The Word (logos) would conceive life within. The water would reveal and release what the Word (logos) had begun. The Spirit would breathe into that new life, giving it movement and maturity.

Nicodemus had read Ezekiel's promise in shadow; Jesus stood before him as the substance.

The prophet foresaw what the Messiah fulfilled:

A cleansed life.

A transformed heart.

An indwelt spirit.

Three witnesses working as one - the Word (logos) planting life, the water revealing it, the Spirit empowering it. Nicodemus hadn't encountered new information that night; he had encountered a new arrangement. What he had memorized as prophecy, he now faced as Person - the very One whose blood would speak what water alone could never say.

But conception, cleansing, and indwelling all leaned toward a final necessity - the blood that speaks, the blood that cleanses, the blood that makes every other witness true.

Born of Water and Spirit

Baptism isn't a bath; it's a birth. The water breaks, and the Spirit breathes. You come up gasping for a world you were always meant to live in. Baptism does not create that life; it delivers what the Word (logos) conceived, what the Father initiated, and what the blood made possible.

That's why Jesus joined the two - water and wind. The Spirit moves where He wills, and the water witnesses what He touches. Together, they complete what the Father initiated, what the Word began, and what the blood authorized.

This is why baptism cannot be reduced to a stage moment, a formula, or a ticket-to-heaven slogan. Birth is too weighty for that. Water and Spirit are not props in a church performance. They stand where God brings forth what He Himself began.

What It Really Means to Be Born Again

This is the pattern of new birth: the Father draws, the Word (logos) conceives, the blood speaks, godly sorrow awakens repentance, the water delivers, and the Spirit breathes. Nicodemus learned that seeing the Kingdom begins with revelation, but entering it requires participation.

The Word (logos) conceives you. The blood claims you. The water delivers you. And the Spirit gives you breath. And where Logos has conceived life, Rhema calls it forth. That is why this birth is not merely inward awakening, but revealed obedience.

Born of Favor, Not Fear

Rebirth isn't a punishment for sinners; it's a promise for seekers. Heaven doesn't drag you into the water; it invites you. Being born again isn't escaping judgment - it's entering relationship. It's not fire insurance; it's divine inheritance.

God's charis - His favoring disposition - draws you, woos you, awakens you. [38] The Father initiates the approach, the Word (logos) plants the seed, and godly sorrow softens the heart until repentance becomes possible. When you finally respond in the way God appointed, heaven calls it birth.

Reflection from the Upper Room

Nicodemus came at night with questions and left carrying revelation.

He didn't need better theology; he needed a new nature - one conceived by the Word (logos), claimed by the blood, and animated by the Spirit.

When Jesus said, *"You must be born again,"* He wasn't describing reform. He was describing resurrection.

The Father had drawn Nicodemus to Jesus, the Word (logos) had pierced him, and now the Spirit hovered over him - waiting for the waters that would one day bring him forth. New birth is not an idea to learn; it is a life to receive.

What heaven conceives, heaven also intends to bring forth. Heaven does not speak in abstractions. It watches over what it says until it stands up in the earth (Jeremiah 1:12). That is why this conversation still troubles shallow religion. It refuses to let new birth remain invisible, abstract, or safely theoretical.

---

[38] For a detailed understanding of God's charis (Grace), refer to Appendix A

Chapter Nine

The Blood That Changed the Water

Water had always been ready. What it lacked was authorization.

Long before rivers ever carried repentance, blood had already marked covenant. The first covenant sign God gave Abraham was not water, but blood - circumcision, a cutting of flesh that sealed promise into the body (Genesis 17:10–11). It was painful, permanent, and unmistakable. Covenant, from the beginning, always required life.

Blood marked belonging. Blood signified inheritance. Blood testified that a life had been claimed by God. [39]

This was not because blood ruled by itself, but because God placed life within it and appointed it to speak where covenant was sealed. *"The life of the flesh is in the blood,"* the Lord declared, *"and I have given it to you upon the altar to make atonement"* (Leviticus 17:11). Blood did not initiate covenant - God did. Blood bore witness to what God had established.

Water would come later - not to replace blood, but to stand beside it.

Every covenant after Abraham followed the same pattern. Blood established access. Water prepared approach. Blood atoned;

---

[39] See Appendix D – The Witness of the Blood

water cleansed. Altars ran red, then hands were washed. The order never changed.

That order matters, because it keeps water in its rightful place. Water was never given the task of establishing covenant. It was appointed to serve what covenant had already made possible.

That is why John's baptism could awaken repentance but could not promise remission. John stood in water, but the Lamb had not yet stood on the altar. His river could call hearts back to God, but it could not yet quiet the conscience. The water was obedient - but it was waiting.

John understood this better than anyone.

"I baptize you with water," he said, *"but One is coming after me…"* (Matthew 3:11).

Water was not enough. Not yet.

Why John Could Prepare but Not Complete

John's baptism was real. It was necessary. And it was incomplete.

People came confessing sins, hearts broken open by godly sorrow. The river carried repentance honestly. But remission - the removal of guilt - required blood. Scripture is unambiguous: *"Without the shedding of blood there is no remission"* (Hebrews 9:22).

Water could wash the body. Only blood, appointed by God, could cleanse the conscience (Hebrews 9:14).

That is why John never claimed finality. His baptism prepared the way; it did not finish the work. He stood between promise and fulfillment, pointing beyond himself to the Lamb whose blood would testify to what water alone never could.

The river was doing everything it had been given to do. It could summon repentance, but it could not yet witness a covenant that had not been ratified in blood.

When the Lamb Entered the Water

Then, the Lamb stepped into John's river.

Jesus did not enter the Jordan to repent. He entered to align. The water received Him, not as a sinner seeking cleansing, but as a Son submitting to the Father's will. This was not water authorizing Jesus - it was Jesus submitting to righteousness and, in doing so, appointing the water as a future witness.

And heaven responded.

The Spirit descended. The Father spoke. The witnesses aligned.

Yet still, no blood had been shed.

Jesus' baptism revealed righteousness. The cross would secure remission.

Between the Jordan and Calvary stood a silence - not emptiness, but anticipation. The water had witnessed obedience. Now it waited for sacrifice. The river had seen repentance before.

What it had not yet seen was the blood that would make its witness covenantally complete.

Commission of Authority

Jesus did not leave baptism in the Jordan. He carried it through the cross, through the resurrection, and then placed it into the hands of His disciples.

After rising from the dead, He spoke with an authority no prophet had ever claimed:

"All authority in heaven and on earth has been given to Me. Go therefore…" (Matthew 28:18–19)

This mattered. Baptism was no longer to be fenced in by a religious class, guarded by priestly hands, or rationed by men who loved titles more than obedience. In Christ, God's people are now *"an holy priesthood"* and *"a royal priesthood"* (1 Peter 2:5, 9), and the risen Lord placed this commission into the hands of His disciples beneath His own authority:

"All authority in heaven and on earth has been given to Me. Go therefore…" (Matthew 28:18–19).

Not to create chaos, but to keep the old gatekeeping spirit from dressing itself in new robes - the same spirit Jesus rebuked when He said, *"Woe unto you, scribes and Pharisees, hypocrites! for ye shut up the kingdom of heaven against men"* (Matthew 23:13; see also Luke 11:52).

The water would not belong to Pharisees, priests, or polished hierarchies. It would belong to the authority of the One who said, "Go." That is why, in Acts, Philip did not wait for temple rank or priestly permission. When the Ethiopian said, "*See, here is water; what doth hinder me to be baptized?*" Philip went down into the water with him and baptized him (Acts 8:36–39).

Baptism did not originate in Acts. Acts is the obedient echo of a command already spoken by the risen King.

The apostles were not inventing a practice - they were executing authority.

What began as submission in the water now flowed outward as commission to the nations. The One who stepped into the river in obedience now sent others into the water with authority.

Obedience had been witnessed. Authority was about to be released. That is the shift. Before the cross, water could prepare. After the cross and resurrection, water could now bear witness under the authority of the One who had fulfilled what it had only shadowed before.

The Cross: When the Blood Testified

At Calvary, everything changed.

The blood that circumcision had foreshadowed was finally poured out - not from the flesh of infants, not from lambs without voice, but from the Son Himself. Covenant was no longer marked outwardly in flesh; it was written inwardly upon the conscience (Hebrews 10:16–22).

The blood did not negotiate forgiveness. It testified that the price God required had been paid.

By God's appointment, the blood spoke peace where accusation once stood (Hebrews 12:24). It bore witness that access had been opened, guilt had been addressed, and reconciliation had been secured.

And when the blood testified, the water was no longer waiting.

From that moment forward, baptism would never again be mere preparation. The river now carried authority - not because water had changed, but because the covenant it witnessed had been completed.

The water could now testify to what heaven had already secured. Water did not become a new savior at Calvary. It remained water. But from that moment on, it no longer stood only in anticipation. It stood in witness to a finished covenant.

Why Baptism Changes After the Cross

This is why baptism sounds different in Acts than it does in the Gospels.

Before the cross: repentance prepared hearts, water awakened longing, remission was still future

After the cross: repentance still turns hearts, blood now testifies to remission, water bears witness to a finished work

Peter could now say what John never could: *"Be baptized… for the remission of sins."* (Acts 2:38)

Not because water suddenly became magical, but because the blood had already borne witness.

The river did not become mystical. It became authorized.

That is why Acts does not speak as though the apostles discovered a better ritual. It speaks as though the witnesses have finally come into their appointed order. Blood has testified. Water can now agree. Spirit can now confirm.

Water Still Witnesses - Covenant Establishes

Water has always remembered God's movements. It has always stood where He acts. But water never establishes covenant - it testifies to it.

God establishes. Blood testifies. Water witnesses. Spirit confirms.

This is the pattern Scripture never abandons.

So when a believer steps into baptism now, the water does not argue forgiveness into existence. It agrees with heaven. It stands alongside the blood and bears witness that this life has entered covenant.

The water does not decide the case. The covenant has already been established.

That is why baptism cannot be reduced either to a bare symbol or to a ticket-to-heaven transaction. It is more than a picture, because God appointed it as witness. But it is not the source of covenant, because covenant was established elsewhere - in blood.

Why This Matters Before New Birth

Before Jesus spoke to Nicodemus about being born of water and Spirit, something had to be settled:

Birth requires blood.

No life enters the world without cost. No child is born without broken water and bloodshed. New creation follows the same pattern. The water may break. The Spirit may breathe. But covenant life must first be secured.

That is why new birth could not fully manifest before the cross. That is why water waited. That is why baptism changes everything afterward.

The Jordan prepared the way. Calvary secured the covenant. Now, the river bears witness.

And only now can birth be spoken of in its full covenantal weight. When the Son of God steps into water, and then sheds His blood, the witness of water is forever changed.

Water was always ready. Blood gave it covenantal speech.

Scripture Index

Chapter Ten

Baptism in the Book of Acts: The Living River

When the Son of God steps into water, He changes it. When the apostles step into water, He uses it. And when the early church met revelation, it kept finding water close behind it.

Luke does not present the early church as obsessed with choreography. He presents a people answering heaven in real time. Again and again, revelation led them to water.

The Day the Crowd Asked the Wrong Question

Pentecost did not begin with doctrine; it began with fire. (Acts 2:1-4). Tongues of flame danced above the heads of ordinary people, and the city shook under the weight of conviction. When Peter finished preaching, (Acts 2:14-36) the crowd didn't ask the question modern readers expect.

They didn't say, *"What must we do to be saved (sōzō)?"* [40] That question would come later, in a Philippian jail cell shaken by an earthquake (Acts 16:30).

On Pentecost, the question was simpler: *"Men and brethren, what shall we do?"* (Acts 2:37)

---

[40] See Appendix H – Sōzō and Soteria: Rescue, Formation, and Inheritance

The Word (logos) had pierced their hearts. The Father had drawn them. (John 6:44) Godly sorrow cracked the stone. (2 Corinthians 7:10) Revelation was turning into responsibility.

Peter answered the only way heaven allows:

"Repent, and be baptized every one of you in the name of Jesus Christ for the remission of sins, and you shall receive the gift of the Holy Spirit." (Acts 2:38)

Repentance turned them. Baptism identified them. Remission released them. The Spirit empowered them. (Acts 2:39)

This was not a mechanical formula. It was alignment - a human heart stepping into the order God had now revealed. (Titus 3:5).

Acts 2:38 is not the origin of baptismal authority - it is the first recorded response to Jesus' commission.

Peter was not issuing a new command. He was applying the authority already given on the mountain in Galilee.

That matters. Acts is not inventing baptism theology from scratch. It is showing what obedience looks like once the blood has spoken, the Son has risen, and authority has been released.

The Meaning of *Sōzō*

Modern Christianity often treats salvation [41] like a passcode for heaven. But the Greek word sōzō doesn't mean "admitted." It means to heal (Luke 8:48), rescue (Matthew 8:25), restore (Mark

---

[41] See Appendix H – Sōzō and Soteria: Rescue, Formation, and Inheritance

5:23), make whole (Luke 17:19) - it is what Jesus did for blind eyes, broken bodies, and raging seas.

Sōzō is not a ticket - it is transformation. It is the restoration of a life back into the favor and order of God.

Biblical saving (sōzō) is not escape - it is restoration.

That's why baptism in Acts is never presented as a stand-alone "salvation plan." - "Get your ticket here for your afterlife destination." It is always part of the unfolding work of new creation (2 Corinthians 5:17) - sometimes appearing before the Spirit, sometimes after, always following revelation, always answering the blood that speaks something better (Hebrews 12:24).

"Redemption is not a rescue from life but a restoration into it." (3)

That is why Acts does not speak like a salesman handing out afterlife guarantees. It speaks like a river carrying people out of old order and into living participation with Christ.

Different Waters, Same Witness

Acts does not read like a textbook or manual. It reads like a river - winding, unpredictable, always moving toward life. Flowing wherever revelation is answered.

In Samaria, the water moved before the wind. Philip preached, the people believed, and they were baptized - but the

Spirit waited until the apostles laid hands on them (Acts 8:5–17). Order shifted, but favor didn't.

On a dusty road, a desert whispered its forgotten memory of rain. A chariot rolled to a stop, a eunuch asked a single question, and prophecy found its puddle: *"See, here is water. What hinders me?"* (Acts 8:26-35) Faith met water, and the desert became a sanctuary.

In Damascus, a blinded Pharisee knelt beneath the hands of an unlikely disciple. Ananias whispered heaven's instruction: *"Arise, and be baptized, and wash away your sins."* (Acts 22:16) Saul entered the water as an enemy; he rose as an apostle. The water didn't erase his past - it released him from its ownership.

In Caesarea, heaven outran tradition. While Peter was still preaching, the Spirit fell on Cornelius' household (Acts 10:44–48). The wind moved first, the water followed, and the apostles learned the river answers God's timing, not theirs.

Beside a quiet riverside, Lydia listened with an open heart, and the current repeated the Exodus story in miniature: a life crossing from bondage into belonging. (Acts 16:14-15)

A jailer screamed into the darkness, *"What must I do to be saved (sōzō)?"* [42] (Acts 16:30). The jailer's question was not an abstract theology. It was a cry for rescue from a man staring death in the face. For a Roman jailer, a prison break meant execution

---

[42] See Appendix H – Sōzō and Soteria: Rescue, Formation, and Inheritance

and often the ruin of his household. (18–20) [43] Paul did not minimize that danger; he answered him in a way deeper than panic could imagine. By sunrise, water splashed against prison walls and a Roman household emerged dripping into the dawn (Acts 16:25–34). [44]

And in Ephesus, disciples who had known John's baptism met the revelation of Christ more fully (Acts 19:1–6). What happened there belongs to its own weighty conversation, but Luke places it in Acts for a reason: revelation does not leave water untouched.

"Revelation always calls us deeper. The river never stops at your ankles."(17)

Different rivers.

Different sequences.

Same Presence.

Same Witness.

Heaven did not abandon order; it revealed that order was deeper than human choreography. The heart mattered, and so did the witness God appointed.

---

[43] Roman custodial law held guards personally accountable for escaped prisoners, often resulting in immediate execution and severe consequences for the household (Keener, 2012; Sherwin-White, 1963).
[44] See Appendix G – Household Baptism

Reflection from the Riverbank

The early believers were not paralyzed by ceremony. When revelation came, they looked for water close enough to obey.

Because once revelation comes, water becomes inevitable.

Heaven never demanded uniformity; it honored unity - hearts aligned with the Word (logos), consciences washed by the blood, bodies surrendered to the water, spirits awakened by the breath of God.

And the river still speaks the same invitation: Come. Step where the witnesses agree. Step where the blood has spoken. Step where the Spirit still moves. Step into the water - the river remembers.

Acts does not give us a rigid chart. It gives us a living river. But the river is not confused. It knows what blood has secured, what water must witness, and what the Spirit confirms.

Scripture Index

- Acts 2:1-4
- Acts 2:14-36
- Acts 16:30
- Acts 2:37
- John 6:44
- 2 Corinthians 7:10
- Acts 2:38
- Acts 2:39
- Titus 3:5
- Luke 8:48
- Matthew 8:25
- Mark 5:23
- Luke 17:19
- 2 Corinthians 5:17
- Hebrews 12:24
- Acts 8:5–17

- Acts 8:26-35
- Acts 22:16
- Acts 10:44–48
- Acts 16:14-15
- Acts 16:25–34
- Acts 19:1–6

Chapter Eleven

When the Shadows Agree- Baptism Fulfilled

Prophetic Correlations: When the Old Waters Meet Acts

The book of Acts is not the beginning of baptism's story - it is the moment the shadows finally met the substance. Every baptism in Acts carries the echo of an older river, a hint of a story whose first chapters were written long before Pentecost.

God has always preached through water. Acts simply reveals what the Old Testament rehearsed.

Repentance & Turning - Noah's Flood Revisited

When the crowd in Acts 2 turned toward Peter with trembling hearts (Acts 2:37–38), their repentance wasn't a new idea; it was a return to the oldest storyline in Scripture.

In Noah's day, the flood washed away corruption so creation could breathe again (Genesis 6–9). And notice something often missed: the first time Scripture shows grief leading to a decisive "turn", it is God Himself. *"It repented the LORD… and it grieved Him at His heart"* (Genesis 6:6–7). That doesn't mean God "made a mistake" - it means He rendered a verdict against a world that had become violent and corrupted, and His response to that turning was not a speech, but water.

Peter later said that this flood *foreshadowed baptism* - not the putting away of dirt, but the appeal of a clean conscience toward God (1 Peter 3:20–21).

Just as the flood marked a new world, repentance in Acts marked a new humanity. The waters of judgment had become waters of mercy. The turning of the heart was the opening of the ark.

Repentance did not begin at Pentecost. Pentecost revealed where repentance had been heading all along.

Remission & Cleansing - Saul and the Priestly Washings

When Ananias said to Saul, *"Arise and be baptized, and wash away your sins"* (Acts 22:16), he was invoking imagery Saul already understood.

Before a priest could enter the Holy Place, he washed - not as ordinary hygiene, but for access (Leviticus 16; Numbers 19). The water did not forgive; it prepared.

Now, in Christ, remission was no longer temporary cleansing. It was permanent access into a Presence that the old priesthood could only approach in shadows. Baptism didn't repeat the Day of Atonement - it revealed what the Lamb had finished.

The water did not create Saul's remission. It bore witness that the persecutor's old claim had been broken and that access now stood open in Christ.

Renewal & New Life - The Red Sea Replayed

When Lydia, the jailer, and their households were baptized (Acts 16:13–34), they were stepping into the same pattern Israel experienced at the Red Sea.

Israel passed through water and left their chains buried beneath the waves (Exodus 14). Paul later said they were *"baptized into Moses in the cloud and in the sea"* (1 Corinthians 10:2).

Baptism does the same: it seals a departure before it reveals an arrival. Slaves become sons. Captives come up covenant people. The old whip-crack of Egypt no longer follows them through the water.

Baptism does the same in witness: it seals a departure before it reveals an arrival. Slaves become sons. Captives come up covenant people. The old whip-crack of Egypt no longer follows them through the water.

Community & Belonging - Circumcision of the Heart

Samaria's baptism (Acts 8:12–17) was more than personal repentance - it was entry into a people.

Under Abraham, circumcision marked covenant identity (Genesis 17). At Sinai, washings prepared a nation to meet God (Exodus 19).

In Christ, the two merged. Paul said baptism is the circumcision made without hands, the cutting away of the old nature (Colossians 2:11–12).

The water did not merely cleanse Samaria - it claimed them. A divided people became one Kingdom family.

The old mark had been in flesh. The new witness reached the conscience and gathered a people in Christ.

Empowerment & Spirit - The Priestly Anointing Renewed

When the Spirit fell on Cornelius' household (Acts 10:44–48), Peter recognized an ancient order being fulfilled.

Priests were always washed before they were anointed (Exodus 29:4–7; Leviticus 8:6–12). Water prepared them. Oil empowered them.

Now the Spirit Himself was the oil, and the Name of Jesus was the authority behind the washing.

The pattern hadn't changed - only the covenant had. The same God who anointed Aaron was now anointing Gentiles.

Caesarea was not a break in the story. It was the story opening wider than men had expected.

Cleansing & Commissioning - Isaiah's Coal in Liquid Form

When Saul was baptized, he wasn't simply being forgiven - he was being sent.

Isaiah's lips were touched with a coal (Isaiah 6:6–8), and the prophet rose commissioned.

Saul's washing was the same moment in a different form. The water cleansed. The Word (logos) called. And the man who entered blind emerged burning with assignment.

Baptism wasn't the end of his story. It was the doorway to apostleship.

Baptism was not the end of Saul's story. It was the doorway through which the old life lost its claim and the new assignment began to burn.

Revelation & Completion - Ephesus and the Jordan Echo

The disciples in Ephesus had been baptized once (Acts 19:1–6). But when fuller revelation arrived, they stepped into the water again - not from failure, but from invitation.

Their second baptism mirrored another second crossing: Elisha crossing the Jordan after Elijah's mantle fell (2 Kings 2:8–14).

Elisha did not re-cross because the first crossing was meaningless. He crossed because inheritance had increased. So it was with Ephesus. Not failure. Fuller revelation. Not erasure. Completion

Inclusion & Validation - Rahab, Ruth, and the Gentile Floodgates

When the Spirit fell upon Cornelius' house before baptism (Acts 10:44–48), Peter stood stunned.

But heaven had been hinting at this for centuries.

Rahab welcomed the God of Israel from her window (Joshua 2). Ruth stepped under His wings by covenant choice (Ruth 1:16–17).

Both were outsiders. Both were embraced. Both became part of the lineage of Christ.

Now, in Acts 10, the same grace that grafted two women into Israel was flooding the nations.

A Gentile household heard the Word (logos), the blood spoke over them, the Spirit fell upon them, and the water agreed with heaven.

Summary

Every baptism in Acts is a prophecy fulfilled. Every river is a memory awakened. Every convert is a continuation of a story that began in Eden, rose in the flood, parted at the Red Sea, flowed through prophets, carried John, and kissed the feet of Jesus in the Jordan.

The waters of Acts are not new waters. They are ancient waters finding their meaning in Christ.

The River That Remembered

None of this began in Acts. The apostles were simply stepping into a conversation older than Israel, older than Moses, older than Eden's exile.

Before Pentecost, there was Noah, finding favor (Genesis 6:8). Before Samaria's revival, there was Israel's Red Sea (Exodus 14:21–31). Before Ananias washed Saul, priests washed before ministry (Exodus 29:4). Before Cornelius received the Spirit, Naaman dipped in the Jordan seven times (2 Kings 5:10–14). Before Ephesus stepped into revelation, Elisha crossed the Jordan into inheritance (2 Kings 2:8–14).

Every ripple was rehearsal. Every washing was whispering the same promise: God begins again in water.

So when Peter cried, *"Repent and be baptized,"* the river didn't hesitate - it had been rehearsing its line since Genesis. The river recognized the rhythm.

Acts did not invent the river. It unveiled what the river had been learning to say all along.

Scripture Index

- Genesis 6:8
- Genesis 6–9
- Genesis 17
- Exodus 14
- Exodus 14:21–31
- Exodus 19
- Exodus 29:4
- Exodus 29:4–7
- Leviticus 8:6–12
- Leviticus 16
- Numbers 19
- Joshua 2
- Ruth 1:16–17
- 2 Kings 2:8–14
- 2 Kings 5:10–14
- Isaiah 6:6–8
- Matthew 8:25
- Mark 5:23

- Luke 8:48
- Luke 17:19
- John 6:44
- Acts 2:1–4
- Acts 2:14–39
- Acts 8:5–17
- Acts 8:26–35
- Acts 10:44–48
- Acts 16:13–34
- Acts 19:1–6
- Acts 22:16
- 1 Corinthians 10:2
- 2 Corinthians 5:17
- 2 Corinthians 7:10
- Colossians 2:11–12
- Titus 3:5
- Hebrews 12:24

Chapter Twelve

One River Many Purposes

When One River Does Many Things

Every river carries more than one purpose. It quenches thirst. It nourishes fields. It moves boats and carves canyons. One current, many callings.

One thing you learn pretty quickly about God is that He loves efficiency. One river, many assignments. One act, a dozen outcomes. One dip, eternal ripples.

It's like He looked at baptism and said, "Why make twelve ceremonies when one good dunk will do?"

Baptism is not a spiritual vending machine - it's a divine multi-tool. It can mark repentance, cleansing, commissioning, belonging, restoration, revelation, and empowerment, and on a good day, it'll even fix that identity crisis you've been carrying since third grade. Not because water is magical, but because God has chosen to gather so much witness into one act.

Same water. Different reasons. One Witness watching over it all.

The Layers in the Water

When Peter preached on Pentecost, he wasn't inventing a new ceremony; he was just dragging every old shadow into the light and saying: "You know all that stuff you've been practicing for 1,500 years? Yeah… this is what it was pointing to."

Repentance like John's wilderness altar call (Matthew 3:2). Cleansing like the priests washing up before work (Exodus 29:4). Renewal like Israel's Red Sea jailbreak (Exodus 14; 1 Corinthians 10:2). Belonging like Abraham's covenant mark (Genesis 17; Colossians 2:11–12). Empowerment like Moses anointing Aaron (Leviticus 8:6–12).

Every meaning stepped into the water that day. And none of them drowned.

In one act, all those symbols collided and were fulfilled. The water of baptism carries layered purpose - it doesn't just erase the past; it connects you to your calling.

The Greek word baptizō doesn't mean sprinkle. It means immerse, submerge, overwhelm - the way life overwhelms you when you realize God has a count of every hair on your head. Mikvah, too, was full-body immersion - and when later traditions traded rivers for droplets, they didn't change what *baptizō* means. [45] [46] (8,21–24)

You don't just go under water. You go under revelation.

---

[45] **Mikveh and immersion:** In Jewish practice, *tevillah* (immersion) in a mikveh is not sprinkling. It is understood as **whole-body submersion at once**, with nothing significant blocking the water's contact with the body (an "interposition"). See Asher Meir, "Yitro: Tevilah – Immersion in a Mikveh" (Orthodox Union, 2008).

[46] Archaeology confirms widespread **Second Temple** use of **ritual immersion baths (miqva'ot)** in Judea/Jerusalem. See Reich's overview of miqva'ot in late Second Temple contexts.

That is why baptism can do more than one thing without becoming twelve different rituals. One river can water a field, carry a boat, cut a canyon, and still remain one river. God is no less capable with baptism than He is with creation.

The Misunderstanding of One-and-Done [47]

Somewhere along the way, people decided baptism had to do just one thing. But the early church never saw it that way. They watched it do whatever heaven needed it to do in the moment.

Sometimes it washed repentance raw. Sometimes it lifted guilt off shoulders like a wet coat. Sometimes it connected strangers into family. Sometimes it cracked open destiny like a stone jar and poured Spirit into places no one expected.

One baptism, many outcomes. Heaven appoints the witness.

And yes, sometimes revelation brought people back to the water - not because the first encounter was meaningless, but because understanding deepened, alignment shifted, and what had once been shadow gave way to fuller light.

The disciples in Ephesus were not rebuked; they were brought into fuller revelation (Acts 19:1–6). It was not a meaningless redo. It was completion under greater light.

"Revelation never leaves you where it found you. It drags you deeper or it isn't revelation." (17)

---

[47] See Appendix C – Sacred Cows

This is also where Hebrews and Ephesians stop being enemies. Hebrews can speak of baptisms in the plural (Hebrews 6:1–2), because Scripture knows a broad water-grammar. Paul can speak of one baptism (Ephesians 4:5), because all those witnesses are gathered into one obedience to Christ. Many functions. One river.

Many Purposes, One Presence

Let's break down what the river does - but not like a doctrinal checklist. More like reading the résumé of someone wildly overqualified for the job.

Repentance - "I'm done with my way."

John started it, Peter confirmed it: *"Repent and be baptized."* (Mark 1:4; Acts 2:38). Repentance begins where your excuses run out.

Every step toward the water is a step away from rebellion.

Remission - "I'm free from what I was."

"Be baptized… for the remission of sins." (Acts 2:38) *"Arise and be baptized, and wash away your sins."* (Acts 22:16)

The blood speaks. The water agrees. Guilt evacuates the premises.

Peter added the fine print: Baptism is *"not the putting away of dirt,"* but *"the answer of a good conscience toward God."* (1 Peter 3:21)

116

The water can't remove sin by itself. But when obedience meets His Name, the water becomes a courtroom where guilt loses its case.

Renewal - "I'm alive for what's next."

Buried with Him in baptism… raised to walk in newness of life. (Romans 6:4)

Baptism is both a funeral and a birth certificate. Goodbye, Pharaoh. Hello, future.

Belonging - "I'm part of something bigger."

"For by one Spirit we were all baptized into one body." (1 Corinthians 12:13) *"As many as were baptized into Christ have put on Christ."* (Galatians 3:27)

This is not baptism into a sect, a brand, or a denomination with a logo and a loyalty test pretending to be the whole body. It is baptism into Christ, and therefore into the people who belong to Him.

Some people join churches by shaking hands. The early church joined the Body by getting soaked.

They went down individuals. They came up a family.

Empowerment - "I'm ready to be sent."

Jesus said, *"You shall receive power when the Holy Spirit comes upon you."* (Acts 1:8)

And notice what that power was **for**: *"and you shall be witnesses unto Me."* (Acts 1:8) They had already cast out devils and healed the sick under delegated authority (Luke 9:1–2; Luke 10:19). Pentecost wasn't God handing them a new set of tricks - it was God clothing them with strength to carry a public testimony that could not be silenced: boldness, endurance, clarity, and a life that preached.

John uses a different word when he says, *"to them gave He power to become the sons of God"* (John 1:12). That "power" is **authority/right** *(exousia)* - permission to belong, to be counted as family. Acts 1:8 is **power/ability** *(dunamis)* - strength to live that family identity as a witness in the world. Authority makes you family. Power makes that family visible.

When He was baptized? *"The heavens opened."* (Luke 3:21–22) Heaven basically tore the roof off and said, 'This One. Watch Him.'

In Acts? Sometimes the Spirit came *with* the water. Sometimes *after.* Sometimes *before.*

Heaven rarely waits to be polite. But water remained the doorway where purpose put on its shoes.

One Lord, One Faith, One Baptism - Many Revelations

Paul wrote that to the same city where disciples had once gone down again under fuller revelation (Ephesians 4:5; Acts 19:1–6). He wasn't contradicting himself. He was clarifying the source:

There is only one true baptism - the one done in obedience to Christ - but its assignments are endless.

Water, Spirit, Fire. Not competing baptisms. Not spiritual power-ups or evolution stages. But the many ways Scripture speaks of God bringing a person under His dealing. Preparation. Presence. Power. Different witnesses. Same Lord.

The mistake is not in seeing many functions. The mistake is in imagining many rival rivers. Scripture gives us one river under Christ, but it refuses to reduce that river to one thin assignment.

Scripture Index

- Matthew 3:2
- Exodus 29:4
- Exodus 14
- 1 Corinthians 10:2
- Genesis 17
- Colossians 2:11–12
- Leviticus 8:6–12
- Acts 19:1–6
- Mark 1:4
- Acts 2:38
- Acts 22:16
- 1 Peter 3:21
- Romans 6:4
- 1 Corinthians 12:13
- Galatians 3:27
- Acts 1:8
- Luke 3:21–22
- Ephesians 4:5

Chapter Thirteen

When Revelation Spreads

When Revelation Becomes Contagious

I remember one service when I was working the altar during worship. A man had come forward, pouring his heart out to the Lord. He'd been raised in church but had wandered deep into drugs and dealing, been arrested, overdosed more than once. That night he told God, *"If something doesn't change, I'm going home to end it."*

I knelt beside him. Remorse was written across his face. He said he'd once felt God call him into ministry, but he'd run - and now he was sure he'd run too far. He thought he'd ruined every chance.

I told him, "If you can still feel His presence, He isn't done with you. You can't outrun the One who never stopped running toward you." Something broke. He began to shake under the weight of conviction and hope. When he finally asked, "What do I do now?" I said, "Repent of the past, and answer what God is doing in you with obedience."

He jumped up. We headed for the changing room. As I waited in the hallway, others began to gather - one, then another, then a line that stretched down the corridor. They hadn't heard our conversation, but something in the room had shifted. A spirit of revelation had settled on the people, and suddenly everyone wanted to respond. Some came broken. Some came hungry. Some came because revelation had suddenly made obedience unavoidable

That night the tank became more than water; it became a ripple of awakening. When revelation touches one heart, it never stops there. It spreads like waves, turning a single act of obedience into a flood of new beginnings.

That does not mean every wave carries the same response in the same way. It means revelation has a way of waking a room. Once heaven starts dealing with one heart openly, others begin to hear the water too.

The Signature of Obedience

In Acts, the miracle never came from the formula. It came from the faith. The Ethiopian didn't ask for a doctrinal chart. He asked, *"Is there water near here?"* (Acts 8:36)

Right question. Right heart. Right river.

Revelation invites. Obedience responds. Transformation happens. Every. Single. Time.

That does not mean obedience is careless. It means it is alive. The early church did not treat baptism like a dead ritual to be filed away. They treated it like a living answer to what God had just made known.

The Power of Revelation Remembered

Priests washed repeatedly when they drew near to minister (Exodus 30:18–21). Israel washed when they approached God (Exodus 19:10). Naaman dipped seven times (2 Kings 5:14) - because apparently his pride was waterproof.

Scripture is not embarrassed by repeated acts of obedience when God appoints them.

But repetition in Scripture is not the same thing as routine ritual maintenance. Not every return to water is baptism, and not every repeated cleansing image should be forced into rebaptism. Sometimes the point is approach. Sometimes preparation. Sometimes purification. And sometimes, when fuller revelation breaks open what was only partly understood before, the river waits there too.

Repetition isn't redundancy. It's refinement.

So if someone says, "I've already been baptized," the next question is not casual and it is not mechanical. It is not "why not get wet again?" It is "what has God actually revealed, and what is this water now being asked to witness?" A soul is not sinning by trembling toward obedience. But those who shame that trembling, or stand between conviction and the water, take on a far more dangerous posture. "What doth hinder me?" is not a question the Church should answer lightly (Acts 8:36). *"Can any man forbid water?"* is not just permission - it is a warning to anyone tempted to stand in the way (Acts 10:47).

The Kingdom's Logic

In the Kingdom, obedience is never wasted motion. Even when you don't understand every detail, your obedience writes a story heaven keeps reading aloud. And you never step into baptism alone; the witnesses step in with you.

Scripture says that every word is established *"in the mouth of two or three witnesses"* (Deuteronomy 19:15; 2 Corinthians 13:1). So when you enter the water, heaven sends three:

- the Water that receives you,

- the Spirit who breathes on you,

- and the Blood that declares your cleansing and covenant (1 John 5:6–8).

Together they testify: *"This life is real. This turning is true. This beginning is established in heaven and revealed on earth."*

And with those witnesses beside you, every purpose of baptism becomes a confession heaven agrees with:

- Repentance says, *"I'm done with my way."*

- Remission says, *"I'm free from what I was."*

- Renewal says, *"I'm alive for what's next."*

- Belonging says, *"I'm part of something bigger."*

- Empowerment says, *"I'm ready to be sent."*

Each purpose is a verse in the same song - one river, many refrains, one step of obedience, many witnesses.

The water receives it.

The Spirit seals it.

The Blood establishes it.

And the Kingdom calls it done.

That is why baptism can carry many purposes without becoming many disconnected ceremonies. The witnesses do not compete. They agree.

Reflection - The River Keeps Expanding

The same Jordan that opened before Joshua as Israel crossed into promise became the pulpit where John cried, "Repent!" The same current in which Naaman the leprous Syrian dipped and came up clean carried the Savior of the world (Joshua 3:14–17; 2 Kings 5:10–14; Matthew 3:1–6, 13–17).

Baptism doesn't change because the water changes. It changes because revelation does.

And revelation, once it starts moving, doesn't stay in its lane. It floods.

So if you ever find yourself wondering - "Why did I get wet?" the river itself will answer: The river of obedience never dries up. It just keeps finding new banks to flood.

"Because something in you was ready to live."

Not every flood is the same flood. Not every washing is the same washing. But when God reveals, water is never far away.

Part Three

Deep Waters

When Motives, Meanings, and Movements Collide

Water marks the moment.

The Spirit fuels the mission.

But fire - fire refines the witness.

Every generation has tried to reduce baptism to a ceremony, a slogan, or a contest of who got it right. But the river keeps slipping past the fences men build for it. Anyone willing to step in, not with perfect wording, but with hearts ready to be searched, stripped, and led deeper, will find His Presence waiting.

Chapter Fourteen

Not Magic Words but Divine Authority

When Words Become Spells

Humans love formulas. Say the right words, in the right way, and God has to move - or so we think. But heaven doesn't respond to pronunciation; it responds to authority.

Baptism doesn't draw its power from the phrase that's spoken; it draws power from the Person it represents. The Greek phrase *"in the name of"* uses the word *onoma*, which carries the sense of "under the authority of." It's not about how the name is pronounced; it's about whose authority you're standing in when you speak it.

When Jesus said, *"All power is given unto me in heaven and in earth…"* *"…Baptize them in the name of the Father, and of the Son, and of the Holy Spirit,"* (Matthew 28:18-19), He was not handing down a recital.

He was transferring authority.

The same authority that raised Him from the dead now stood behind every baptism performed in His name.

That is why Acts never argues about wording. Authority was settled before the first convert ever entered the water.

If baptism were a linguistic formula, then we'd all have to use the original Greek or Aramaic to make it "work." That's not

Christianity - that's incantation. That's the language of cults, not covenants.

Heaven never taught spells; it taught surrender. The power isn't in the syllables; it's in the submission.

Quick (and slightly hilarious) historical note: the apostles didn't baptize anyone using the modern English letter **J** (n.d.) [48]. The New Testament writes His name in Greek as *Iēsous*, and English did not even separate **I** from **J** until long after the apostolic age. So, the first believers were never relying on English phonetics to make heaven listen. They spoke His name in the languages they had, and heaven answered all the same. That should calm a few people down immediately. The early believers spoke and wrote His name in the languages they actually had, and heaven responded all the same. Which is the point: this isn't incantation. It's authority (26)[49] [50].

The Language of Power

If baptismal power depended on the *spoken formula*, we'd all need perfect accents and the correct vowel length from first-

---

[48] **Encyclopaedia Britannica.** (n.d.). *J*. In *Encyclopaedia Britannica*. Retrieved February 21, 2026.

[49] **Chisholm, H.** (Ed.). (1911). *J*. In *Encyclopaedia Britannica* (11th ed.). Cambridge University Press. (Reprinted/hosted at Wikisource; retrieved February 21, 2026.

[50] For centuries, **I** and **J** weren't even treated as separate letters in the Latin/English tradition - what we now print as *J* was a later spelling development. Before this, the name Jesus did not exist.

century Galilee. But Jesus wasn't teaching phonetics - He was commissioning authority.

Formulas belong to magic. Authority belongs to the Kingdom. And Scripture reinforces this through the witness pattern: the Water, the Spirit, and the Blood agree on earth (1 John 5:8). None of them depend on pronunciation. Authority is recognized by obedience, not diction. Heaven hears alignment long before it hears articulation.

Incantations say, "Say it right, or it won't work." The Gospel says, "Obey in faith, and heaven will confirm it."

That's why Paul could baptize Gentiles in Greek, Peter could baptize Jews in Aramaic, and both were heard in heaven without subtitles. Authority translates; formulas don't. This is the difference between magic and mandate.

And that is exactly why the church gets into trouble whenever it starts treating the river like a microphone test: check the wording, check the volume, check the accent, and maybe heaven will sign off. No. Heaven is not waiting for better phonics. Heaven is looking for obedience under the authority of the risen Christ.

Authority, Not Articulation

Heaven recognizes submission, not syllables. Demons didn't tremble because Peter's grammar was correct; they trembled because he carried Christ's commission. That's what baptism is - an act of embodied obedience to divine authority.

It's not your public announcement; it's your spiritual alignment.

Romans joins belief in the heart with confession made known (Romans 10:9–10). But baptism is not just another way of speaking. It is obedience enacted. Confession is faith made known; baptism is your body's surrender.

When Jesus said, *"Baptize them in the name of the Father, and of the Son, and of the Holy Spirit,"* (Matthew 28:19) He wasn't handing out a recital script. When Peter said, *"Be baptized in the name of Jesus Christ,"* (Acts 2:38) he wasn't editing the script. They were both declaring the same authority - the authority of heaven expressed through Christ.

What gives the Name its authority isn't pronunciation - it's covenant. Heaven doesn't respond to vowels; it responds to the Blood. Jesus isn't Lord because we say His Name loudly enough. He is Lord because He poured out His blood, rose in power, and was given *"the Name above every name"* (Philippians 2:9–11).

The Blood established the covenant.

The Name enforces the covenant.

The Spirit witnesses the covenant.

That's why 1 John 5:8 says the Spirit, the water, and the Blood agree.

Water can witness obedience.

Spirit can empower obedience.

But only the Blood authorizes it.

That is the whole point. Water is not out here freelancing. It stands under covenant. It witnesses what blood established, what Spirit confirms, and what obedience answers.

The Formula Myth

The early church never stood at the river policing pronunciation. They didn't argue over who said what over whom. They simply obeyed, and God responded.

The idea of a "correct formula" came later - when religion began trusting ritual more than relationship. We turned baptism into courtroom language instead of covenant language. But God isn't impressed by recitation; He honors revelation.

If power depended on perfect speech, then no translation could carry authority. The same God who hears prayer in every tongue can recognize obedience in any language.

Heaven isn't moved by formula because heaven is the One who starts the process. No one comes unless the Father draws them (John 6:44). No heart opens unless the Word (logos) plants the seed (James 1:18; 1 Peter 1:23). No conscience breaks unless godly sorrow cracks the stone (2 Corinthians 7:10). And no soul rises toward life (zoē) unless the Word (rhēma) is heard as a living summons - awakening faith and pulling the feet toward obedient washing in the water (Romans 10:17; John 6:63). The *rhēma* doesn't do the washing. It *calls you to it.* The water bears witness to the response (Ephesians 5:26).

By the time someone steps into the water, the conversation was already started in heaven. Baptism doesn't activate God - it answers Him.

That alone should bury the spell-theory. Spells try to force heaven to act. Baptism answers what heaven already began.

The Commission Behind Peter's River

Peter's river didn't carry "extra power" because Peter had a better phrase.

It carried weight because Peter had been authorized.

John preached repentance in the Jordan. Jesus entered that water to fulfill righteousness and appoint baptism as a future witness. But Acts didn't invent baptism - Acts obeyed what Jesus commissioned.

After rising from the dead, Jesus didn't hand out a pronunciation guide. He announced jurisdiction:

"All authority in heaven and on earth has been given to Me. Go therefore…" (Matthew 28:18–19)

That's the missing link many arguments skip. Without that moment, Peter's preaching is just passion and Peter's baptizing is just activity. But with that moment, every baptism in Acts is an act of delegated authority - not human ritual.

Matthew 28 is the mandate. Acts 2 is the execution.

And here's where the church has tripped for centuries: we turned two complementary texts into competing scripts.

Jesus says, *"baptize them in the name of the Father, and of the Son, and of the Holy Spirit"* (Matthew 28:19). Peter says, *"be baptized… in the name of Jesus Christ"* (Acts 2:38).

Some readers treat that like a contradiction. Others treat it like a debate bracket. But Scripture isn't teaching a formula contest - it's showing authority expressed and authority applied.

Matthew 28 identifies the source of the authority - the Father's will, revealed through the Son, made effective by the Spirit. Acts identifies the King whose authority is being obeyed - Jesus Christ, the One to whom all authority has been given.

So the "Name" isn't syllables. It's jurisdiction. The question isn't *how it was said*. The question is *whose authority is being obeyed*.

One text gives the commission in its full horizon. The other shows that commission obeyed in history. They do not fight each other. They finish each other's sentence.

A Quick Laugh at a Bad Idea (So We Don't Accidentally Teach It)

Now… if we wanted to misread Scripture the way religious people sometimes do, we could try this:

- "Matthew 28:19 makes disciples."
- "Acts 2:38 remits sins."

- "So if you want both, you need both phrases, in the correct order, with the correct accent, and preferably in King James."

Congratulations - we just reinvented baptism as a spell.

That's not the heart of the Bible. That's Hogwarts with a hymnal.

Because disciples aren't made by reciting titles over water. Disciples are made by teaching, training, and obedience - which is exactly what the Commission says: *baptize… teaching them to observe all things…* (Matthew 28:20).

And remission isn't produced by a "Jesus Name" soundbite. Remission is blood-authorized - and baptism is the covenantal witness that answers what the blood has secured. Water doesn't purchase cleansing. Water testifies that cleansing has been granted.

So no - Matthew doesn't "make disciples" by a phrase, and Acts doesn't "remit sins" by a phrase.

The Cross, by the Blood, secures remission.

The risen Christ issues the Commission and delegates authority.

The apostles (and disciples) carry out the command in faith and obedience.

The Spirit, the water, and the Blood bear witness in agreement.

Why We Need Both Passages Without Turning Them Into Rival Teams

Here's the truth that keeps the reader out of the ditch:

- Matthew 28 without Acts becomes a commission with no obedience - authority with no execution.
- Acts 2 without Matthew 28 becomes execution with no mandate - activity without stated authorization.

You need both, not as competing formulas, but as a complete picture:

Authority given → command issued → obedience offered → witness established.

That's why Peter's river has weight. Not because Peter "found the right wording," but because Peter stood inside the authority of the risen Christ and carried out what Jesus had already commanded.

So when the church argues "Titles vs. Name," it's often arguing about the wrong thing.

Scripture isn't asking, "Did you say it perfectly?" Scripture is asking, "Did you obey under Christ's authority?"

And heaven has never needed subtitles to recognize obedience.

Who's Running the Dunking Booth?

And while we're on the subject, let's roast one more cow - the one that insists only ordained ministers can baptize.

Jesus didn't limit baptism to clergy; He commissioned believers. *"Go therefore, and make disciples of all nations, baptizing them…"* (Matthew 28:19). He didn't say, *"Only if you've got a license."* He said, *"If you believe, go and do."*

The right to baptize doesn't come from an organization; it comes from authorization. All that's required is belief and alignment with the authority of the One who sends. Jesus never gave His servants permission to build a gate around the water. He forbade the kind of hierarchy that turns service into status and commission into control (Matthew 23:8–12; Luke 22:25–26). Kingdom order is real, but no man-made system gets to claim ownership of Christ's command. What God arranged for function, men must never corrupt into rank and control.

In Acts 8, Philip wasn't an apostle when he baptized the Ethiopian. He was a believer under authority. That's the only credential heaven checks.

If clergy were the only ones allowed to baptize, the revival in Acts would have collapsed by chapter four. The Gospel spread too fast for apostolic scheduling. Heaven designed baptism for believers, not bureaucrats. The authority flows from Jesus to disciples, to new disciples. Anyone who obeys the commission may carry the commission.

So if someone says, "You can't baptize unless you're ordained," just smile and ask, "Who's running your dunking booth - men or God?"

Because when believers operate under divine authority, heaven recognizes the act every time. Some men only trust water when it is administered by the polished, the titled, and the approved. Heaven is not so easily impressed. God has always been more interested in obedience than optics.

That does not mean authority is casual. It means it is delegated. The river is not lawless. It is governed from a higher throne than the church office.

Why Heaven Honors Authority

Authority isn't about rank; it's about relationship. When Jesus submitted to John's baptism, heaven opened - not because John had status, but because Jesus stepped into alignment. When you step into the water under the same authority, heaven still opens.

Jesus stepped into John's water, but He carried heaven's Blood. When He rose out of the river, the Spirit descended because the Witnesses were aligning - Water receiving, Spirit descending, and Blood soon to be poured out.

That's the same agreement 1 John 5:8 says still happens when *you* enter the water. Authority isn't a badge you wear - it's a witness you stand under. That's what "in the name of" (*onoma*) means - not a phrase you pronounce, but a power you carry. Not magic words, but divine authority, as we mentioned at the beginning of this chapter.

The same Spirit that descended on Jesus descends on you. The same Voice that said, *"This is My beloved Son,"* still says, *"This is My beloved child."*

Not because the river became a spell, but because the covenant stands, the Blood speaks, and heaven still recognizes what is done under the Son's authority.

Reflection - Heaven's Signature

The power of baptism isn't in how you say it; it's in Who signs it. Heaven never notarized a formula. It only witnesses obedience. The water doesn't respond to language; it responds to lordship.

The water doesn't respond because you spoke the Name correctly. It responds because the Blood gave that Name its throne, the Spirit bears witness to that throne, and you stepped into the water under that authority.

Heaven never honors formulas. Heaven honors covenant.

Scripture Index

- Deuteronomy 19:15
- Matthew 17:5
- Matthew 28:18–20
- Matthew 28:19
- Mark 16:16
- John 6:44
- Acts 8:12–17
- Acts 8:35–39
- Acts 9:17–18
- Acts 10:44–48
- Acts 16:30–33
- Acts 22:16

- Romans 6:3–4
- Romans 10:9–10
- 2 Corinthians 7:10
- 2 Corinthians 13:1
- Philippians 2:9–11
- James 1:18
- 1 Peter 1:23
- 1 Peter 3:21
- 1 John 5:6–8

Chapter Fifteen

The Baptism of Belonging: When the Water Builds Family

The Water That Made Us Kin

I've seen it more than once - a baptism service where strangers became siblings. No last names. No labels. Just joy. Something happens in that moment when a person steps into the water and the church holds its breath. Heaven calls them *family*, and earth can feel it.

Every baptism is a birth announcement - not just to heaven, but to a family that didn't know it was missing a piece. It's the moment when the Kingdom grows by one and the body becomes more complete.

Because no one is born again without being born *into* something. Every birth has a home. Every newborn needs a family.

When Jesus spoke of being *"born of water and of the Spirit"* (John 3:5), He was describing more than a mystical rebirth - He was describing adoption.

In adoption, someone must call your name before you can call theirs. That is why Scripture says no one comes unless the Father draws them (John 6:44). Adoption begins with the Father's desire, is authorized by the Blood, made visible in the water, and sealed by the Spirit. Paul said we receive *"the Spirit of adoption, whereby we cry, 'Abba, Father'"* (Romans 8:15). Baptism isn't just rebirth - it is the moment the Father claims you publicly, and the Spirit teaches you the language of belonging.

In the ancient world, adoption was not sentimental; it was legal, binding, and lifelong. A child adopted into a household took the family name, inherited the father's rights, and carried the family seal. That's the image Paul drew when he wrote,

"As many of you as were baptized into Christ have put on Christ." (Galatians 3:27)

Baptism is heaven's covenant witness of belonging. The water does not create sonship, but it stands there testifying: *"This one is mine they belong here now."*

Before there was a Christian baptism, there was a Jewish mikveh - the immersion that marked a Gentile's conversion to Judaism. Rabbis used to say, *"He who has become a proselyte is like a newborn child."* (Reich, 2013). That was the rhythm Jesus stepped into at the Jordan. When He came up from the water and the Father's voice thundered,

"This is My beloved Son, in whom I am well pleased," (Matthew 3:17). Heaven was not adopting Jesus - it was openly declaring the Son who had always been the Son. This was not a change of identity but a public attestation of who He was - royal, prophetic, and unmistakable (Psalm 2:7; Isaiah 42:1).

The Spirit descending was not sentiment - it was witness. The same three witnesses that John said agree on earth (1 John

5:8) stood around Jesus in that moment: Water receiving Him, Spirit resting on Him, Blood already promised in covenant. Every believer's baptism echoes that same courtroom of witnesses.

And every time someone rises dripping from the water, that same declaration echoes again. Heaven calls their name, wraps them in belonging, and introduces them to a family that has been waiting for them all along. Baptism doesn't just wash away the past - it welcomes the adopted into their new inheritance.

Not by making them sons apart from Christ, but by bringing them into the Son in whom that inheritance lives.

The Family That Found Each Other

When we pastored a church full of new believers, they wanted to be together all the time. Every weekend there was a cookout, a bonfire, or a trip to the lake. They'd call us and say, "Pastor, we're having barbecue again - you have to come."

At first, I thought it was just enthusiasm - the excitement of early faith. But one evening around the fire, one of them said something that stayed with me:

"We lost all our old friends when we were born again. You're all we have now."

That's when it hit me. Baptism hadn't just washed away their past; it had woven them into a new family. The water that separated them from who they were had also joined them to who they were becoming - together.

They didn't just find a church; they found a home. And
every meal, every laugh, every shared prayer was another reminder
that we had all been born again into the same household of faith.[1]

A Family, Not a Franchise

Rick Warren once said that when God gives new life, He
doesn't send newborns into the wilderness - He sends them into a
nursery.[2] You weren't born again to wander. You were born again
to *belong*.

In *Cultivating the New Nature*, Kevin Rice wrote that
"spiritual formation requires a family where growth is modeled
and maturity is nurtured." [3] That's what the church is supposed to
be - not a franchise, but a family; not an organization, but an
organism.

David Webb echoes this in *Building the Kingdom Through the
Local Church*:

"The local church is God's training ground for the
Kingdom, where sons and daughters learn to reign together."[4]

That's what baptism initiates - *a shared life, not a solo walk.*

The river is not a private achievement unlocked. It is a
threshold crossing into a people.

The Covenant That Connects Us

Baptism doesn't just cleanse - it connects. It's the water of
covenant that makes strangers into kin.

Paul said,

"For by one Spirit we were all baptized into one body." (1 Corinthians 12:13)

And again,

"As many of you as were baptized into Christ have put on Christ… you are all one." (Galatians 3:27–28)

Baptism doesn't join us to a denomination; it joins us to a divine bloodline. The Blood names us. The water identifies us. The Spirit seals us. This is why Paul says the Spirit Himself bears witness with our spirit that we are children of God (Romans 8:16). Baptism is not a membership ritual - it is a family verdict.

Heaven doesn't see church membership; it sees covenant membership. One Lord. One faith. One family.

Heaven didn't just adopt you - it introduced you to your siblings.

The Water That Levels the Ground

When the early believers gathered for baptism, there wasn't one pool for the rich and another for the poor. Unlike the mikveh traditions reserved for elite Jewish sects, the slave and the scholar descended the same steps and rose the same way - soaked, equal, and smiling.

The water didn't care about their reputation. It only cared about their willingness to surrender.

The water has one requirement - humility. The rest gets washed away.

The Jordan River doesn't remember titles, only testimonies. Baptism levels the ground beneath every foot that steps in. The proud come low. The broken rise whole.

That may be one of the river's holiest habits: it makes brothers out of people who would never have sat at the same table before they got wet.

Community Through Cleansing

Every act of cleansing in Scripture was an invitation back to community. In ancient Israel, a leper wasn't just healed; he was *restored to the camp*. The unclean weren't washed to isolate - they were washed to return.

The mikveh - the Jewish ritual bath - symbolized re-entry into fellowship. So when Jesus and His apostles called people to baptism, it wasn't just a call to repentance; it was a call to *relationship*. The newly baptized in Acts *"continued steadfastly in fellowship"* (Acts 2:42). The water didn't just wash them - it wove them together.

Baptism was never about escaping sin; it was always about entering fellowship. The Gospel does not save people into a vacuum. It saves them into a body.

Belonging by Water, Blood, and Spirit

John wrote,

"There are three that bear witness on earth: the Spirit, the water, and the blood." (1 John 5:8)

The blood makes us family by redemption. The water identifies us with that family by covenant. The Spirit empowers that family by indwelling.

Together, these three witnesses speak one truth: *we belong to Him and to one another.* The cross gave us kinship by blood. Baptism gave us kinship by water. The Spirit gives us kinship by breath.

And every time we gather, we breathe the same air of grace, favor, and purpose. That is why isolation has always been a lie. The witnesses do not testify to lone survivors. They testify to a household.

Breaking the Isolation Gospel

We live in a world where faith is often sold as a solo act. "Me and Jesus" has replaced "we and the Kingdom." But Jesus didn't die to build an audience - He died to build a body.

Baptism isn't the mark of your independence; it's the sign of your interdependence. You can't be baptized into isolation. You can't walk out of the water and say, "I don't need the church." Because the moment you come up, you're already surrounded.

Baptism doesn't happen in a mirror; it happens in a body.

If you came up out of the water still thinking you're alone, you missed the miracle standing next to you. The river does not produce freelancers. It produces family.

Living Wet Together

Belonging isn't a feeling; it's a practice. To live "wet" is to remember the water that connected you - to keep washing one another in grace. [51]

Jesus told His disciples,

"If I then, your Lord and Teacher, have washed your feet, you also ought to wash one another's feet." (John 13:14)

We live "wet" when we forgive. We live "wet" when we serve. We live "wet" when we remind one another of who we really are.

Every act of mercy, every prayer of intercession, every meal shared among believers - these are all echoes of that same water. Baptism begins the fellowship; discipleship keeps it flowing.

Every time you forgive, you prove the water is still working.

The river does not end at the tank. It keeps running through kitchens, hospital rooms, prayer circles, and gravesides - anywhere the family of God remembers how to carry one another.

---

[51] See Appendix A: Word Study Spotlight – CHARIS (grace)

Reflection – The Sound of Shared Water

We all came to the water alone, but none of us came up alone. The cry that rises from newly baptized hearts - that sudden sense of "Father" - is not emotion but inheritance. It is the Spirit of adoption awakening your first word as a family member (Romans 8:15–17). You rose from the water with a new vocabulary: belonging.

Adoption is not a feeling you grow into; it is a verdict spoken over you. The Father draws, the Blood authorizes, the water identifies, and the Spirit seals. Paul said we receive "the Spirit of adoption, whereby we cry, 'Abba, Father'" (Romans 8:15). That cry isn't taught - it's inherited. You don't learn to belong; you awaken to it. When you rise from the water, the first breath you take is borrowed from the One who calls you His.

The same Spirit that filled your lungs filled mine. The same water that washed your past washed mine. The river we entered separately now flows through us together.

We are one current. One body. One family.

That is the sound of shared water: not strangers standing politely in the same room, but sons and daughters learning they were always meant to come home together.

Scripture Index

- John 3:5
- John 6:44

- Matthew 3:17
- Romans 8:15

- Romans 8:16
- Romans 8:15–17
- Galatians 3:27
- Galatians 3:27–28

- 1 Corinthians 12:13
- Acts 2:42
- John 13:14
- 1 John 5:8

Chapter Sixteen

Baptism of Fire - When the Water Isn't Enough

When Heaven Strikes a Match

The story of God is a story of fire. He lit the bush that burned but was not consumed (Exodus 3:2). He filled the night sky over Israel's tents with a pillar of flame (Exodus 13:21-22). He answered Elijah's prayer on Mount Carmel with fire that consumed everything - even the stones (1 Kings 18:38).

When heaven wants to make something holy, it doesn't just wash it - it burns it clean. John the Baptist said it clearly:

"I indeed baptize you with water unto repentance, but He who comes after me is mightier than I… He will baptize you with the Holy Spirit and with fire." (Matthew 3:11)

Water cleanses. Spirit empowers. Fire transforms.

But fire does not fall at random. Heaven does not ignite what heaven has not first claimed. What the Blood has redeemed, what water has witnessed, and what the Spirit has filled, fire now refines.

Fire is not another baptism in the sense of another ritual - it's the *manifestation* of the one already received. It is what happens when the Spirit who fills you begins to *refine* you. When the presence that once hovered now inhabits. The same Spirit that descended like a dove on Jesus descended like fire on His followers. Same power, new purpose.

The dove and the flame do not fight each other. One marks belovedness. The other marks habitation.

When the Upper Room Ignited

Pentecost wasn't spontaneous; it was sequential. The Blood had already spoken, the new covenant had already been inaugurated in Christ's sacrifice, the grave had already lost its argument, and now the risen Christ poured out the His Spirit to inhabit what redemption had made clean.

They had obeyed. They had believed. They had already been baptized. But Jesus told them to *wait* - not for another ceremony, but for the *promise of the Father.* (Acts 1:4)

So they gathered - one hundred and twenty hearts in an upper room, praying between promise and fulfillment. And when the day of Pentecost fully came, heaven broke its silence:

"There came a sound from heaven, as of a rushing mighty wind… and there appeared unto them cloven tongues like as of fire, and it sat upon each of them." (Acts 2:2–3)

That was the baptism of fire. Not spectacle - substance. Not a new religion - a new reality. The same Spirit that hovered over creation now hovered over people, turning their fear into boldness. Fire fell where obedience waited.

Not because they had learned the right trick, but because the house was ready, the promise was ripe, and heaven had decided to move in.

When God Moves In

When God dwells somewhere, fire follows. In the wilderness, He moved into a tent - and fire came out from before the Lord and consumed the offering (Leviticus 9:24). In Jerusalem, He moved into a temple - and fire came down from heaven and filled the house (2 Chronicles 7:1–3). At Pentecost, He moved into people, and cloven tongues like fire rested upon them (Acts 2:3).

Every time heaven finds a home, it lights a match. Scripture says *our God is a consuming fire* (Hebrews 12:29; Deuteronomy 4:24), so when He makes a home, He doesn't only ignite it, He purifies what He inhabits.

David wanted to build God a house, but God told him, *"I have not dwelt in houses made with hands"* (2 Samuel 7; Acts 7:48). He was waiting for the day He could dwell in living temples - hearts made clean, bodies made His (2 Corinthians 6:16; 1 Corinthians 3:16; Ezekiel 36:26–27). That is what happened in Acts 2. It was not a visitation; it was habitation. And the fire was the proof.

Paul said Christ sanctifies His people *"with the washing of water by the word (rhema)"* (Ephesians 5:26). He was not describing two separate cleansings, nor was he suggesting that Scripture (*logos*) replaces obedience.

In Scripture, *logos* (the Word as eternal record) is the preexistent Word - Jesus Christ through whom life is conceived (John 1:1–4; James 1:18; 1 Peter 1:23). *Rhema* (the Word as revealed utterance) is that same *logos* heard, unveiled, and responded to in time. *Rhema* does not replace water; it summons obedience toward it. Revelation always calls for response.

So the Word (rhēma) does not "wash" the inward man - it awakens him. It wounds what is hard, softens what is proud, convicts what is hidden, and births faith in the hearer (Jeremiah 23:29; Hebrews 4:12; Romans 10:17; 2 Corinthians 7:10). It breaks up fallow ground so a new heart can be received (Hosea 10:12; Ezekiel 36:26). But the cleansing that removes guilt and purifies the conscience belongs to the Blood, not the syllables (Hebrews 9:14; Hebrews 9:22; Hebrews 10:22).

What the Word (*rhēma*) awakens, baptism answers.

The water is not the cleanser; it is the covenantal witness that answers the Word (*rhema*) already at work. Obedience is what "breaks the water" - the moment revelation (*rhema*) becomes response, and conception (*logos*) steps into birth.

The Blood authorizes that moment. [52] The Spirit indwells it. The water agrees with both.

That is why Scripture says the Spirit, the water, and the Blood bear witness together (1 John 5:8). The Word (*logos*)

---

[52] See Appendix D – The Witness of the Blood

conceives life. The Word (*rhema*) awakens the heart. The water identifies the crossing. The Spirit takes up residence.

One cleansing. One covenant. One family. Conceived by the Word (*logos*), summoned by the Word (*rhema*), witnessed in the water, inhabited by the Spirit.

The baptism of the Holy Ghost is when God moves in. The baptism of fire is when God makes Himself at home.

One fills you; the other refines you. One indwells; the other reveals. One empowers; the other consumes whatever competes with His presence.

The first says, "I am here." The second says, "Now everything in this house answers to Me."

The Pattern of Fire

From Genesis to Pentecost, God has always moved in the same rhythm. First the cleansing. Then the indwelling. Then the fire.

This wasn't a new lesson; it was the same pattern Scripture had been rehearsing for centuries. Jesus spoke it plainly to Nicodemus, water and Spirit as the doorway into Kingdom life (John 3:5–8). But Israel had already lived the shadows: purification that restored readiness to approach (Numbers 19), cleansing before service, then glory filling the house (Exodus 40:34–35), and fire coming from the Lord to mark what He had claimed (Leviticus 9:24; 2 Chronicles 7:1–3). The Upper Room didn't invent the choreography, it fulfilled it. It was the old choreography finally finding its living bodies.

Before a priest ever touched holy things, he stepped into water. The laver waited for him in the outer court, silent but essential. Only after the washing came the Presence. Only after preparation came habitation. (Exodus 29:4)

When Moses finished the tabernacle, Israel saw this pattern unfold again. The last peg was driven into the ground, the last curtain sewn into place - and then the cloud descended. The glory did not visit; it moved in. (Exodus 40:34) Cleansing made room. Indwelling claimed the room.

When Aaron lifted his hands and blessed the people, when obedience had met order and sacrifice had met altar, *fire came out from before the LORD*" and consumed the offering. (Leviticus 9:24) It was the same in Solomon's day: the temple was dedicated, the prayers were offered… and fire fell again. (2 Chronicles 7:1)

The fire wasn't punishment. It was confirmation. It was God saying, *"I receive this house, and I fill it."*

That pattern never changed; it only became personal.

At Pentecost, the disciples were not random targets of divine flame. They had been washed - not merely by water, but by repentance, surrender, and obedience. They had been marked by promise, for Jesus breathed on them and said, "Receive the Holy Spirit" (John 20:22), not as the final Pentecost outpouring, but as a prophetic preview of the indwelling that was about to arrive. And then, when the house was in order and the hearts were aligned, the fire came.

Not to destroy. To dwell.

Tongues of fire rested on each of them because heaven was declaring the same message spoken over every Old Testament altar: *"This place belongs to Me."* But now the altar was not stone - it was flesh, a body prepared for dwelling (Hebrews 10:5, 1 Corinthians 3:16, John 1:14). The temple was not a building - it was people.

Fire didn't fall on the unbelievers outside. It fell on the believers inside. Because fire is not drawn to rebellion; it is drawn to readiness.

This is still the pattern: Cleansing prepares you. The Spirit inhabits you. And the fire reveals what the cleansing made possible and what the Spirit now empowers.

The fire of God never comes to destroy His dwelling place. It comes to illuminate it.

When the Spirit Comes, Something Shows

In Samaria, believers were baptized in water, but the Holy Spirit hadn't yet fallen until Peter and John laid hands on them - and something visible happened (Acts 8:14–18). Simon saw it and wanted to buy it. At Cornelius's house, the Spirit fell *while Peter was still preaching,* and everyone heard them speak with tongues and magnify God (Acts 10:44–46). At Ephesus, after they were rebaptized in Jesus' name, the Spirit came upon them, and they spoke with tongues and prophesied (Acts 19:6).

Different places. Same power. Every time, heaven made it plain enough to be noticed. In every scene, the fire confirmed what the water and Spirit had already witnessed.

Tongues were the first language of the fire. Not as a badge of rank, but as the evidence of overflow. Heaven spoke through human mouths because the house was not just cleansed and claimed, it was inhabited.

That is why the fire cannot be reduced to emotional noise. Fire leaves evidence. Not always the same evidence in every life, but never nothing.

The Fire's Purpose

Fire doesn't come to entertain; it comes to transform.

When the Spirit fills you, He brings comfort. When the fire baptizes you, He brings combustion.

The baptism of fire doesn't just make you emotional - it makes you effective. It burns away mixture, compromise, and apathy. It separates your calling from your comfort.

Isaiah saw it in vision: a coal from the altar touched his lips, and he cried, *"Woe is me, for I am undone!"* (Isaiah 6:5–7) Then came the voice: *"Now go."* Cleansed lips, commissioned heart. That's the fire.

Fire as Refinement, Not Judgment

For the believer, fire is not punishment - it's partnership. It's God saying, "If I'm going to live here, I'll clean and decorate the house Myself."

"Our God is a consuming fire." (Hebrews 12:29)

That's not a threat; it's an invitation. Because if He consumes, He cares. If He burns, He's close enough to touch.

The fire doesn't burn you *up*; it burns you *through*. It purifies motives, passions, and purposes until what's left looks like Jesus. God's fire does not consume His children; it consumes everything that contradicts the Blood that redeemed them.

Malachi saw it coming:

"He shall sit as a refiner and purifier of silver... and He shall purify the sons of Levi." (Malachi 3:3)

The fire doesn't visit; it abides. It stays until the reflection of the Refiner appears in the silver.

From Tongues to Transformation

Tongues are not the goal of the fire; they're the beginning. The greater evidence of the baptism of fire isn't a sound but a surrender. It's a life that glows with obedience and flickers with favor.

Peter went from denying Christ to declaring Him before thousands (Luke 22:25-62; Acts 2:14-41). That's the baptism of fire. The same mouth that once cursed in fear now burned with courage.

When the fire truly falls, timidity becomes testimony. The fisherman becomes a flame.

When Fire Falls Again

The baptism of fire didn't end in Acts. It still descends on any altar built from hunger and humility. It finds hearts that are tired of religion and ready for reality.

Every revival in history has begun with the same combination: Repentance made the altar; hunger called the flame. (27–31) [53] [54] [55] [56] [57] Scripture keeps showing the same rhythm: repentance prepares the heart (Acts 3:19), and hunger reaches for more of God than bare religion can provide (Matthew 5:6). And when hunger and thirst catch heaven's attention, things get filled.

If the Holy Ghost is God in you, then the fire is God revealed through you.

---

[53] Revival Fire: How God Can Use You to Win Souls and Change Hearts. Duewel, Wesley L. (1988)
[54] They Found the Secret - V. Raymond Edman (1956)
[55] God's Generals - Roberts Liardon (1996)
[56] When God Comes to Church - Raymond C. Ortlund Jr. (2009)
[57] Charles G. Finney, Lectures on Revivals of Religion (1835), teaches that revival begins when "repentance breaks up the fallow ground" and "fervent desire for God invites His presence."

And when the world sees a believer burning but not consumed, they stop to watch - and maybe, like Moses, they turn aside to hear the Voice speaking from the flame.

That is when witness stops being theory. A burning life will always preach louder than a polished one.

Reflection

You were washed by water, filled by Spirit, and now you burn with the fire that proves you belong (Titus 3:5-6; Acts 2). Fire is the Spirit's way of finishing what water began.

The goal isn't to be wet or loud; the goal is to burn - to live as a lamp the world can't ignore.

Water marked the beginning. Fire reveals the depth of what began there.

Scripture Index

- Acts 1:4
- Acts 2
- Acts 2:2–3
- Acts 2:14–41
- Acts 3:19
- Acts 7:48
- Acts 8:14–18
- Acts 10:44–46
- Acts 19:6
- 1 Corinthians 3:16
- 2 Corinthians 6:16
- 2 Samuel 7
- 1 John 5:8
- 1 Kings 18:38
- 2 Chronicles 7:1–3
- Ephesians 5:26
- Exodus 3:2
- Exodus 13:21–22

- Exodus 29:4
- Exodus 40:34
- Ezekiel 36:26–27
- Hebrews 4:12
- Hebrews 12:29
- Isaiah 6:5–7
- Jeremiah 23:29
- Leviticus 9:24
- Luke 22:25–62
- Malachi 3:3
- Matthew 3:11
- Matthew 5:6
- Titus 3:5–6

Part Four

The Flame and the Fellowship

Water makes you clean. Fire makes you courageous.

Chapter Seventeen

Living in the Fire: When the Flame Finds Fellowship

When the Flame Refuses to Stay in the Upper Room

The fire of Pentecost was never meant to stay upstairs. It spilled down the steps, out the doors, into the streets - and into ordinary people who couldn't keep quiet anymore (Acts 2:47)

The same flame that filled the upper room refused to stay there; it *"gave them great power"* as they spread the gospel (Acts 4:33), and *"the Lord added to the church daily"* wherever the fire traveled (Acts 2:47).

Fire is not a rival baptism. It is what happens when obedient surrender comes fully alive.

The same Peter who once denied Jesus now preached with boldness. The same disciples who hid behind locked doors now faced crowds and councils. Because when fire touches fear, it doesn't negotiate - it consumes it.

The baptism of fire is not a single flash of emotion. It's the ongoing ignition of a life fully yielded. It's the Spirit reminding flesh that courage is contagious. [58]

The upper room was never meant to become a museum. It was a furnace meant to send burning people into the world.

---

[58] See Appendix E – The Witness of the Spirit

Fire That Travels

Everywhere the early believers went, sparks flew. At Samaria, the gospel jumped cultural boundaries. At Ephesus, sorcerers burned their scrolls (Acts 8:5-8; Acts 19:17-20). At Little Rome, as Philippi was known, prisoners sang until walls shook (Acts 16:25-26).

The fire moved because hearts moved. Baptized people carried embers in their obedience. You can't quarantine the kind of Presence that chooses humanity as fuel. Fire is never a fourth witness; it is the Spirit's witness made visible (1 John 5:6-8).

When heaven found a body to burn through, the world found a light it couldn't put out.

That is the trouble with real fire: it refuses to stay private. It leaks into cities, prayer meetings, prison cells, marketplaces, and dinner tables.

The Two Temperatures of Fire

Fire both purifies and propels. It purifies what can stay and propels what must go.

Purifying Fire – exposes motives, refines intentions, burns away mixture. *"He will sit as a refiner and purifier of silver."* (Malachi 3:3)

Propelling Fire – launches mission, drives witness, compels compassion. *"His word was in my heart like a burning fire shut up in my bones."* (Jeremiah 20:9)

When you receive the baptism of fire, the same flame that cleanses you also commissions you. The altar and the platform become the same piece of ground.

That is what religion keeps trying to separate. It wants altar-fire without assignment, or assignment without altar-fire. God insists on both.

Not Emotional Heat, but Holy Heat

Some confuse fire with frenzy. Noise isn't proof of flame. Real fire leaves residue: purified conscience, fearless compassion, and a tenderness toward people that feels almost impossible.

The baptism of fire is not about volume; it's about velocity - the speed with which obedience follows revelation. When the Spirit says, "Go," fire doesn't argue; it moves.

Emotion may flicker, but fire endures.

Anybody can get loud. Fire is what stays after the room gets quiet.

How Fire Manifests

In Scripture, fire revealed itself through tongues, prophecy, boldness, generosity, endurance. In modern life, it still does. Fire may sound like prayer at midnight, or forgiveness that costs you something. It may look like courage in conversation, or mercy that refuses to quit.

You know the fire is still burning when obedience is faster than fear.

The baptism of fire produces visible fruit:

- A heart quick to repent.
- A mouth quick to bless.
- Hands quick to serve.
- Feet quick to go.

That's how the Spirit's flame turns disciples into witnesses. Not performers. Not religious pyrotechnics. Witnesses.

Keeping the Flame

Every fire needs fuel. The early believers kept theirs through prayer, fellowship, breaking bread, and remembering. (Acts 2:42) We keep ours the same way.

Prayer is oxygen. The Word is a lamp. Hunger is the kindling. Obedience is oil (Psalm 119:105).

"Is not My word like fire?" says the Lord (Jeremiah 23:29). Scripture keeps the flame alive because it carries the spark that first ignited us.

This is why Paul told Timothy, *'Stir up the gift of God which is in you'* (2 Timothy 1:6). The word Paul uses carries the idea of rekindling, fanning a fire back into flame. Flames don't keep themselves; they are tended.

166

The flame of God never dies from persecution - it dies from neglect. Feed it, and it will illuminate everything around you. Ignore it, and darkness grows confident again.

Revival isn't God returning; it's believers remembering. The Lord does not need waking up. We do.

When Fire Meets Fellowship

Fire burns brightest in community (Hebrews 10:24-25). Coals separated grow cold, but pressed together, they glow. The baptism of fire isn't given to create superstars; it's given to create unity.

When the early church prayed together, *'the place was shaken'* (Acts 4:31). Fire multiplies when believers gather. This is why Scripture urges us not to forsake gathering, but to "stir up one another" in faith (Hebrews 10:24–25). Coals burn brighter together.

Each flame at Pentecost rested upon them, but together those flames became a fireplace for the nations. That's why the Spirit still gathers us - not to show off gifts, but to sustain warmth.

A single torch can light a path. A gathered fire can warm a people. God seems to like both, but He rarely settles for the first alone.

When the Fire Fell in the Prayer Room

I remember attending a conference in a large city where one of the ministers I deeply respected was scheduled to speak. Before service, a few of us gathered with him for about an hour. He told stories of how God had moved through him in the gifts of the Spirit. It wasn't boasting; it was fire retold.

When we finally left to let him prepare, I walked down the hallway into the prayer room the church had opened for the event. I began to pray that God would anoint the man I had just met, that the service would be saturated with His presence.

As I prayed, the atmosphere shifted. The air thickened with holiness; voices began to rise. People were praying in other tongues, some softly, some with urgency. Then a spirit of travail settled over the room - low groans, tears, deep intercession.

I heard one woman in particular, weeping and rocking with her knees drawn up, two others holding her hands. There was a brightness around her - an almost tangible light that seemed to pulse with the rhythm of her prayer. As I turned toward her, the Lord spoke to my heart:

"When Zion travails, sons and daughters are born into the Kingdom." (Isaiah 66:8)

I knew then what was about to happen in that service wasn't just a sermon - it would be a birth. The fire of God's Spirit was about to sweep through that house. What began as prayer would become travail, and what began as travail would become *transformation.*

That's what the baptism of fire looks like when heaven touches earth - light breaking through ordinary rooms, hearts ignited in unity, and spiritual sons and daughters born through the flame of intercession.

Fire does not always arrive looking dramatic. Sometimes it comes as burden. Sometimes, as groaning. Sometimes, as the unbearable sense that heaven is about to push something living into the world.

Living as the Lamp

Jesus said, *"You are the light of the world."* (Matthew 5:14) He wasn't handing out compliments; He was handing out assignments.

Fire makes you luminous so others can find their way. A lamp doesn't brag about its flame; it simply refuses to hide it. *"That you may shine as lights in the world."* (Philippians 2:15) When your life burns with obedience, someone else finds direction.

The baptism of fire turns believers into beacons - not perfect, but persistent; not loud, but luminous.

Flames don't compete; they complete each other's glow.

From Cleansing to Commission

Water washes. Spirit fills. Fire sends.

Each baptism unfolds into the next until the believer becomes the message itself. When water, Spirit, and fire agree, you don't just attend revival - you become it.

That's the pattern: Cleansed to carry. Filled to overflow. Burned to become. For we are living sacrifices, set apart and aflame (Romans 12:1; 2 Corinthians 3:18).

The river got you ready. The flame gets you moving.

Reflection – The Flame That Follows

The fire didn't fall once; it keeps falling. It falls on obedience. It falls on hunger. It falls on humility.

The same God who kindled the bush in the desert still ignites hearts in cities and living rooms.

And when He does, the sound isn't thunder - it's transformation.

The truest fire leaves more than noise behind. It leaves people who burn steadily enough to light the way for somebody else.

Scripture Index

- Acts 2:42
- Acts 2:47
- Acts 4:31
- Acts 4:33
- Acts 8:5–8
- Acts 8:14–17
- Acts 16:25–26
- Acts 19:6
- Exodus 3:2
- Exodus 13:21–22

- Hebrews 10:24–25
- Isaiah 66:8
- Jeremiah 20:9
- Jeremiah 23:29
- Malachi 3:3
- Matthew 5:14
- Philippians 2:15
- Psalm 119:105
- 2 Corinthians 3:18
- 2 Timothy 1:6
- Romans 12:1
- 1 John 5:6–8

Chapter Eighteen

When Revelation Requires a Return

When Revelation Outgrows Ritual

Some people treat baptism like a punch card.

Got wet? Check the box. Put the date in your Bible. Never speak of it again.

But rivers don't flow once and quit. And revelation doesn't either.

Sometimes what God shows you *after* your first baptism makes you realize that your next step isn't rebellion - it's revelation. The heart that once obeyed a little now wants to obey a lot. And when revelation grows, obedience has to catch up (James 4:17).

This chapter is not arguing for endless repeats, emotional maintenance, or ritual recycling. It is arguing that when fuller revelation arrives, or when a life returns from open rupture into open surrender, Scripture does not treat the river as closed. Sometimes the first obedience was real, but partial. Sometimes the first surrender was true, but immature. And sometimes the next step is not denial of the former - it is obedience to the light now given.

Rebaptism, then, is not casual. It is not for every stumble, every mood swing, or every troubled week. But neither is it forbidden territory every time the river is mentioned again.

When Paul Met the Soaked but Still Searching

Paul found this out in Ephesus. He walked into a group of disciples who had already done *something* with what they'd heard. They weren't rebels; they were responders. They had been baptized into John's message - repentance, readiness, a heart turned toward the coming King (Acts 19:1–3; Mark 1:4).

But when Paul asked, *"Did you receive the Holy Spirit when you believed?"* they answered, *"We have not so much as heard whether there is a Holy Spirit."* (Acts 19:2)

They had obeyed what they knew. But what they knew belonged to an earlier threshold.

So Paul didn't scold them. He brought them into fuller revelation.

John's baptism, he explained, was a baptism of repentance, *"telling the people that they should believe on Him who would come after him - that is, on Christ Jesus."* (Acts 19:4)

In that moment, their revelation widened. What they'd done was real - but it belonged to an earlier chapter. They had embraced preparation; now they were being invited into fulfillment.

And how did they respond?

"When they heard this, they were baptized in the name of the Lord Jesus." (Acts 19:5)

They didn't argue. They didn't say, "But we already did that *John* thing." They simply went back to the water.

And this time, when they came up, the Spirit came down (Acts 19:6).

That is the center of this chapter. Not insecurity. Not superstition. Not religious repetition for its own sake. Fuller light arrived, and the river was asked to witness that fuller light.

The Completion Principle

That's the secret of Acts 19: Rebaptism wasn't correction; it was completion. Not rejection of the first step, but expansion into the next one.

They hadn't been wrong. They had just been early.

Every revelation carries an invitation (Psalm 119:130). Every invitation deserves a response (Acts 10:33).

New light doesn't cancel old obedience; it completes it.

And heaven help the one who stands in the way. If God is calling a person back to the water, no one has the right to shame them back onto the shore. When a soul asks, "What doth hinder me?" (Acts 8:36), the Church should tremble before it answers. Peter did not ask, "Who can criticize this?" He asked, "Can any man forbid water?" (Acts 10:47). The one who mocks honest obedience does not defend truth; he risks becoming a stumbling stone in the path of revelation. Better to bless a trembling yes than to stand on the bank and argue with a river God is still using.

The river does not shame the first step. It simply agrees when heaven calls for the next one.

When the River Calls You Back

Some believers treat baptism like a wedding photo - proof that something real happened *once*.

Scripture treats it more seriously than that. There are moments when what was once entered in shadow must later be answered in fuller substance.

Naaman dipped seven times in the Jordan before his skin was made new (2 Kings 5:14). That is not Christian rebaptism, and we should not pretend it is. But it does tell us something important: Scripture is not scandalized by repeated water-obedience when God appoints it. The miracle was not in the number. It was in the obedience (2 Kings 5:11–13).

The miracle wasn't in the number; it was in the obedience. So if heaven pulls on your heart and points to the water again, it's not because your first baptism "didn't work." It's because your understanding has grown (Proverbs 4:18), and your Father refuses to waste that growth.

If the river calls you back, it's not because you failed the first swim - it's because there's more current waiting for you.

Heaven is not offended by deeper surrender.

When the Clean Get Dusty

Of course, sometimes it isn't *new* revelation that calls us back - it's the need for *new* mercy.

Even the washed still walk dusty roads.

Jesus told His disciples, *"He who is bathed needs only to wash his feet, but is completely clean."* (John 13:10)

The bath speaks of redemption; the feet speak of fellowship.

You don't get born again/enter the family over and over again, but your walk still needs washing.

Some wander after the water. Old habits sneak back in. The "old man" that baptism buried tries to claw his way out of the grave (Romans 6:6; Galatians 5:17).

What do you do when that corpse stirs?

You bring it back first to the cross that redeemed you (Romans 6:3–4), to confession, to repentance, to restored fellowship, and to the mercy that still speaks.

John wrote to *believers*, not unbelievers: *"If we confess our sins, He is faithful and just to forgive us our sins and to cleanse us from all unrighteousness."* (1 John 1:9)

Sometimes that cleansing is a prayer in a quiet room. Sometimes it's a tear at an altar. And sometimes, for some people, especially where rebellion was open, departure was decisive, and return is now public and surrendered, the river may also be asked to bear witness.

Rebaptism for restoration is not the church's first answer to every failure. But neither must it be dismissed as superstition whenever a prodigal comes home and asks the water to witness the return. In such cases, the issue is not covenant maintenance. It is open surrender after open rupture.

The River That Refuses to Shame You

The prodigal's story doesn't end in the pigpen; it ends in the Father's arms (Luke 15:20–24). The robe still fits. The ring still waits. The shoes still shine like they did the first day.

The same is true when a believer steps back toward baptism after a season of wandering.

Heaven doesn't roll its eyes and say, "Really? Again?"

It runs.

God is not keeping a tally of how many times you've been under the water. He's listening for one thing: Are you turning toward Me? (Zechariah 1:3; James 4:8)

God doesn't track your submersions; He tracks your surrender.

That is what makes this chapter bearable. We are not talking about religious obsession. We are talking about the mercy of a Father who is not embarrassed when surrender returns dripping.

A Story from the Second Splash

I once had someone come to me after service and say,

"Pastor, I know God touched me when I was baptized years ago. I felt His presence. But now I finally understand what I was stepping into. I want to be baptized again - not because I doubt it, but because I see it."

That is the right reason.

The first time, she obeyed conviction (John 16:8). The second time, she obeyed understanding (Luke 24:45).

We filled the tank again.

When she came up out of the water, there was no thunder, no choir of angels - just a deep, heavy peace (Isaiah 26:3; Philippians 4:7) that rolled through the room like a soft current. You could feel heaven hovering over the room.

It wasn't a redo.

It was a response to fuller light.

It did not feel like she was erasing her first "yes," but more like heaven was finishing a sentence it had started years before (Philippians 1:6).

Humor Break – Heaven's Water Budget

Some folks act like heaven is rationing water.
As if Gabriel's in the back room saying, "Careful with that hose, Michael. Kirkland's already had three baptisms. We're going to run out."

Relax.

The river of life has never had a drought (Revelation 22:1). Grace (charis)[59] is not on backorder (Romans 5:17). God is not pacing the throne room, wondering how to stretch the water supply.

If revelation pulls you toward the tank again, go (Acts 22:16).

God isn't short on water.

He's rich in welcome (Ephesians 2:4–5).

The real question is never whether heaven can spare the water. The real question is whether we can bear to let obedience look untidy when revelation deepens beyond our categories.

The Ripple You Don't See

Every act of obedience makes a ripple (James 1:22–25).

The first time you obeyed, it changed your direction. The next time, it might change your destiny.

You can't go back to who you were (2 Corinthians 5:17), but you *can* go deeper into who He's making you to be (Ephesians 4:13–15).

Revelation + obedience = movement.

When revelation widens, and obedience says "yes" again, the river starts to move in fresh ways in you, and around you (Psalm 1:3).

---

[59] Refer to Appendix A

You may only feel the splash, but heaven is already watching the current downstream.

Reflection – The River Never Forgets

The first baptism washed what you knew then (Acts 2:38; Romans 6:4). The next one may bear witness to what you know now (Acts 19:4–6).

The river never forgets your name (Isaiah 43:1).

It only remembers the sound of surrender.

So if heaven whispers, "Come back," don't argue.

Don't overthink it.

If your heart is softer (Ezekiel 36:26), your understanding deeper (Proverbs 2:6), your repentance real (2 Corinthians 7:10) - and the river is being asked to witness fuller light or a public return from real rupture - then yes, it may be time to get wet again.

The Witnesses still agree (1 John 5:8). And the river still knows how to answer surrender.

Scripture Index

- Acts 2:38
- Acts 8:14–17
- Acts 19:1–6
- Acts 19:1–3
- Acts 19:2
- Acts 19:4–6
- Acts 19:5
- Acts 22:16
- 1 Corinthians 3:16
- 2 Corinthians 5:17
- 2 Corinthians 7:10
- Ephesians 2:4–5

- Ephesians 4:13–15
- Galatians 5:17
- Hebrews 10:1
- Hebrews 10:26
- Hebrews 10:29
- Isaiah 26:3
- Isaiah 43:1
- Isaiah 55:1
- James 1:22–25
- James 4:8
- James 4:17
- John 7:38
- John 13:10
- John 16:8
- Luke 15:20–24
- Luke 24:45
- Mark 1:4
- Proverbs 2:6
- Proverbs 4:18
- Psalm 1:3
- Psalm 23:3
- Revelation 22:1
- Romans 5:17
- Romans 6:3–4
- Romans 6:6
- Titus 3:5
- Zechariah 1:3
- 1 John 1:9
- 1 John 5:8

Chapter Nineteen

When the Motive Gets Muddy

When Water Meets a Wounded Heart

Baptism is honest. It never lies for you. It covers what you surrender, but it exposes what you hide. Scripture says the Word (logos) discerns *"the thoughts and intents of the heart"* (Hebrews 4:12), and baptism simply makes that discernment visible.

The goal is cleansing, but the truth is that water also reveals. *"Every way of a man is right in his own eyes, but the LORD weighs the hearts."* (Proverbs 21:2). It shows what we came for. Some come for healing. Some come for holiness. And some… come for attention.

The miracle is that God still lets us all in the same water.

That should make us humble, not suspicious. The point of this chapter is not to teach the church to stand at the river with crossed arms and narrowed eyes. It is to remind us that heaven is not fooled by performance, and yet still merciful to the broken who come mixed, messy, and half-aware of what they are carrying.

The Woman Who Found the Water but Missed the Point

There was a woman in a congregation I once pastored. She came to a service and had a genuine encounter with the Lord. Her story was heartbreaking - years of abuse, trauma, and loss. She'd grown up in a pastor's home and walked far from God.

After service, she came to me with tears in her eyes and said,

"Pastor, I want to be baptized. I want to start over."

We baptized her that night. When she came up from the water, something real happened - she began worship with freedom. She was radiant. We all rejoiced.

But a few months later, her attendance started to fade. I began hearing stories - she was visiting other churches, telling her testimony, and being baptized again and again. Not for cleansing. For clout.

Each time a church held a baptism service, she'd show up, share her story, cry, and go under again. Not because of revelation - because she'd learned that tears draw attention.

Before long, she wasn't seeking transformation - she was chasing validation. The water was still telling the truth; her motive was not.

That's when I learned something that's stayed with me ever since: The water will always witness honestly - but it will not baptize self-deception into surrender.

John the Baptist ran into the same thing. Crowds lined up at the Jordan not because they were repentant, but because revival had become the fashion of the week. When he saw them coming without intention to change, he didn't celebrate their attendance - he confronted their motives.

"Bring forth fruit meet for repentance." (Matthew 3:8) John wasn't trying to thin the crowd; he was trying to deepen the sincerity. He knew what we eventually learn: the water can receive a body, but it will not testify to a lie. Luke's account says the same crowd came for spectacle, not surrender, and John warned them plainly that *"every tree which does not bear good fruit is cut down"* (Luke 3:7–9). Baptism does not demand fanfare; it reveals whether repentance has born fruit.

Isaiah diagnosed the same problem generations earlier: *"This people draw near with their mouth…but their heart is far from Me"* (Isaiah 29:13).

Simon the Sorcerer's Wet Ambition

She reminded me of Simon the Sorcerer in Acts 8. He watched the apostles lay hands on believers and saw the Spirit fall with power. And he thought, *That's the kind of power I could use.*

So he did what many still try to do - he treated the sacred like a shortcut.

"Give me also this power, that on whomsoever I lay hands, he may receive the Holy Ghost." (Acts 8:19)

Simon had already believed and been baptized under Philip's ministry (Acts 8:13). But belief without surrender can still produce counterfeit fruit. He didn't want relationship; he wanted results. He wasn't hungry for God; he was hungry for recognition.

And Peter called him out with surgical precision:

"Your heart is not right in the sight of God." (Acts 8:21)

Simon got in the water, but not into alignment. He went under with ambition and came up with the same motive – because water does not override what pride keeps defending.

He wanted the miracle, not the meaning. Jesus warned of this very temptation: *"Beware of practicing your righteousness before men, to be seen by them"* (Matthew 6:1). And that's the danger of misplaced desire - power without purpose becomes manipulation, not ministry.

The water may receive you, but the witnesses - Spirit, water, and Blood - only agree when the heart aligns with truth (1 John 5:8). Heaven never signs off on counterfeit surrender.

When purpose is lost, power is abdicated.

For the Lord Himself says, *"I search the heart and test the mind"* (Jeremiah 17:10); motive matters before miracle.

Heaven doesn't empower performance; it empowers purpose. That's why God guards motive - not to withhold power, but to preserve its purity.

When the Witnesses Read the Heart

Scripture first lays down the principle that a matter is established by the mouth of two or three witnesses (Deuteronomy

19:15; Matthew 18:16; 2 Corinthians 13:1). So when John says there are *"three that bear witness on earth: the Spirit, the water, and the blood - and these three agree in one"* (1 John 5:8), he is invoking the language of testimony. What we often miss is that these witnesses do not agree with our intent; they agree with God's truth.

The water receives your body, the Spirit discerns your motive, and the Blood testifies to covenant reality. As Paul wrote, *"He who searches the hearts knows the mind of the Spirit"* (Romans 8:27).

Heaven's witnesses cannot be bribed by performance.

This is why Peter told Simon, *"Your heart is not right before God"* (Acts 8:21). The water had accepted him, but the Witnesses had read him. They testified - not to the act he performed - but to the motive he carried.

The writer of Hebrews says the Word (logos) Himself *"discerns the thoughts and intents of the heart"* (Hebrews 4:12). And baptism is one of the places where that discernment becomes visible.

When a heart enters the water in surrender, the Witnesses testify for you. When a heart enters the water in self-promotion or deceit, the Witnesses testify to the truth - not to the performance.

The water never lies. The Spirit never flatters. The Blood never negotiates. For *"man looks on the outward appearance, but the LORD looks on the heart"* (1 Samuel 16:7).

They do not condemn - but they refuse to agree with a motive that contradicts repentance.

Baptism is alignment, not theater. And the Three Witnesses always tell the truth.

That is sobering, but it is also merciful. Better to be read honestly by heaven than applauded falsely by men.

The Crocodile Rule

A friend once told me,

"You can dip a crocodile in holy water, but it'll still bite you when it comes out."

And he was right. Baptism isn't behavior modification; it's spiritual transformation. If you go in pretending, you'll come out pretending - just wetter.

I've also heard the darker version of that joke: "You can baptize a dog, but that doesn't make it a Christian." I hate that line because it turns people into punchlines, and it tempts us to play judge. We're not called to be *fruit inspectors* at the waterline. Fruit takes time to grow, and Jesus said it will be known in season (Matthew 7:16). Paul warned, "Judge nothing before the time… until the Lord comes" (1 Corinthians 4:5). Our assignment is simpler and holier: baptize the repentant who come, then disciple them, walk with them, and let the Witnesses tell the truth.

God doesn't honor the act without the heart. He told Israel long ago, *"I desire mercy, not sacrifice"* (Hosea 6:6). God has always valued motive above motion. He's not after applause; He's after alignment.

That's why motive matters. While baptism can witness cleansing and surrender, it can't wash away deceit. The water responds to surrender, not to showmanship.

The church's job is not to become paranoid. It is to remain honest. There is a difference.

Mercy for the Misguided

Before we get too smug, let's be honest - we've all gone into the water with mixed motives at some point. Maybe we wanted to impress our family. Maybe we were afraid of what others would think if we didn't. Maybe we wanted the feeling, not the formation. Not the kind of formation men manufacture, but the kind produced through repentance, obedience, time, and conformity to His image (Romans 8:29, John 14:15, Luke 9:23).[60]

And yet, in His mercy, God still meets us there. Because even half-hearted steps toward Him still move in the right direction. Because *"a broken and contrite heart, O God, You will not despise"* (Psalm 51:17).

He meets us in the mess, not the performance.

The good news is that while water can reveal your heart, it can also renew it. Scripture calls us to *"draw near to God… purify your hearts… humble yourselves"* (James 4:8–10). Renewal is always available where humility flows. God doesn't disqualify you for

---

[60] For a fuller treatment of formation as covenantal obedience within the life of the local church, see David Webb, **Building the Kingdom Through the Local Church**.

getting it wrong the first time. He just invites you to get it right the next time.

That is where this chapter bends back toward hope. The river is honest, but it is not cruel. It tells the truth in order to heal, not humiliate.

The Heart Always Comes Up Wet

The purpose of baptism isn't perfection. It's purity of heart. It's not the ritual that saves; it's the revelation that transforms.

If your motive is mixed, the water will expose it. If your motive is sincere, the water will sanctify it.

Baptism is God's mirror - and mirrors don't lie.

The same water that cleanses can also clarify.

That is not a threat. It is an invitation to stop pretending before the One who already knows.

Reflection – When the River Reads You

The water never lies. It knows when you're pretending. It knows when you're desperate.

But it never condemns you - it just calls you deeper.

Because baptism isn't about proving who you are; it's about discovering who He is.

The river can't fix a false motive. But it can invite a real one.

John called his generation to honest repentance because the river was never meant for theater (Matthew 3:7–10). That hasn't changed. The river still reads you before it receives you. And true repentance still leaves its fruit, *"earnestness, eagerness, indignation, longing, zeal"* (2 Corinthians 7:10–11), the kind of fruit the river recognizes.

The river is not fooled by spectacle, but neither is it frightened by desperation. Bring it your truth, and let the Witnesses agree with that.

Scripture Index

- Acts 8:13
- Acts 8:19
- Acts 8:21
- Hebrews 4:12
- Hosea 6:6
- Isaiah 29:13
- James 4:8–10
- Jeremiah 17:10
- Luke 3:7–9
- Matthew 3:7–10
- Matthew 3:8
- Matthew 6:1
- Proverbs 21:2
- Psalm 51:17
- Romans 8:27
- 1 Samuel 16:7
- 2 Corinthians 7:10–11
- 1 John 5:8

Chapter Twenty

Baptism as a Lifestyle

The Daily Drowning

Paul once said, *"I die daily."* (1 Corinthians 15:31) That's not a morbid confession; it is the baptismal pattern still working itself out in a living man. Every sunrise gives you another chance to lay the old self down and breathe new life in again.

Baptism was never meant to stay trapped in your memory. It was meant to shape your reflexes. Each new act of obedience remembers that first washing - when the Name of the Lord met the water and sin lost its hold. It's a posture, not a past tense. Every time you choose forgiveness over bitterness, you are living what the water first witnessed. Every time you choose faith over fear, you are walking in the life that came up with you.

Baptism is not a ceremony; it's a pattern - a rhythm of dying and rising, forgiving and being forgiven. Didn't Jesus teach us to pray, *"Forgive us our sins as we forgive those who sin against us"?* (Luke 11:4) And after His resurrection, He breathed on His disciples (John 20:22) and said, *"If you forgive anyone's sins, they are forgiven"* (John 20:23). Every breath of mercy you release is another resurrection in motion.

This chapter is not arguing that the body must be rebaptized every morning. It is saying that the life once witnessed in baptism must keep showing up in how you walk.

Every Shower Is a Reminder

Sometimes I joke with people and say,

Every shower is a baptism reminder - hot water, higher purpose.

Because honestly, life splashes us with all kinds of grime. You don't stay clean by remembering your last bath; you stay aware by living near the flow.

When that first rush of water hits your shoulders, whisper a little prayer:

"Wash my mind again, Lord. Rinse off yesterday's worry. Let me walk out of this bathroom new again."

You'll be surprised how spiritual a simple shower can feel when you treat it like a sacred metaphor. Not because the water itself holds power, but because your heart remembers the One who washed you first.

The shower is not a sacrament. It is a reminder. The point is not to make the bathroom a baptistry; it is to keep the soul from forgetting what the baptistry meant.

Micro-Immersions

Every day carries small obediences that echo the water. When you repent - that's a rinse. When you pause before reacting - that's patience washing its hands before it touches someone else. When you thank God in traffic instead of honking your theology - that's sanctification with seatbelts.

The priests did not go back through consecration every morning, but they did wash their hands and feet before service. That is the better picture for daily life. You do not get born again every afternoon. But if you are going to touch people, carry peace, speak for God, and serve without spreading yesterday's grime, then something in you has to stay washed.

If you go to the bathroom and never wash your hands, nobody calls that freedom. They call it nasty. Life is full of necessary contact with a fallen world, but what you pick up there should not be what you hand to the next person. Daily repentance, daily mercy, daily surrender - these are the priestly washings of people who intend to touch other lives without defiling them.

You don't need a preacher and a pool for every moment of surrender; you need awareness and obedience. These small obediences echo the same death-and-rising your baptism declared.

A life baptized in purpose doesn't wait for Sunday services; it drips holiness on Wednesday mornings.

The Wet Way to Walk

Living baptized means living aware - aware that you're not who you were yesterday. Grace (God's favor) [61] didn't just meet you once; it walks with you. You don't *keep yourself* clean; you *stay* clean by staying close.

In the Old Testament, priests washed before ministry, not to erase sin but to reset focus. Jesus lived this rhythm Himself -He entered the river once, but He carried its posture into daily life, even kneeling to wash feet so His disciples would learn that cleansing isn't an event but a lifestyle. That's what daily yieldedness does: it resets you. Reminds you that you're not performing for God's approval - you're partnering with His purpose.

John 13 matters here. The bath and the foot-washing are not the same thing. The once-entered cleansing and the ongoing walk-cleansing belong together, but they are not interchangeable.

The Puddle Principle

Children understand this better than theologians. Give a kid a puddle and you'll see pure joy. They don't analyze depth or doctrine; they just jump.

Somewhere between childhood and adulthood we traded splashing for strategy. But maybe holiness looks more like laughter

---

[61] See Appendix A: Word Study Spotlight – CHARIS (grace)

than stiffness. Maybe God still smiles when His kids play in the puddles of His presence.

The Kingdom of heaven belongs to those who aren't afraid to get their shoes wet. Not careless. Childlike. There is a difference, and the river knows it.

Living Wet Means Living Light

The freshly baptized always look lighter - not because the water changed their weight, but because obedience lifted their burden.

Living wet means refusing to carry what God already washed away. It means letting His mercy renew you as often as His Word (logos and rhema) corrects you. (Ephesians 5:26; Hebrews 4:12) It means walking through the world without letting its dust define you.

When shame whispers, "You're still dirty," answer, "I've already been through the water today." Not because you were rebaptized this morning, but because the truth of that water is still answering shame now.

Humor Break - The Back-Row Baptist

One Sunday a man came up after service and said,

"Pastor, I don't think I'm ready for baptism yet. I'm still working on myself."

I told him, "That's like saying you won't take a shower until you're clean." He laughed, then booked a date for next week. Sometimes theology is as simple as hygiene.

Religion waits for perfection. Relationship just hands you a towel.

The Kingdom is not built by people who finally got themselves polished enough to obey. It is built by people who finally got tired of staying dirty.

Dying Daily, Rising Gratefully

Each evening you can rehearse your baptism again: Lay down - die to the day. Rise up in the morning - resurrected into purpose.

The rhythm never gets old because the mercy never does. It's not repetition of the act; it's renewal of the pattern. The Spirit does not drag your body back through a tank each day, but He does keep bringing your attitudes, affections, and responses back under the life your baptism declared.

You can't outgrow obedience; you can only out-refresh it.

Living baptized means living awake to the Spirit's flow - ready to let go, ready to rise, ready to keep answering the life God already began.

Reflection – The Flow That Never Stops

I have learned to live dripping.

To keep the scent of the river on my soul.

To let repentance rinse my pride and gratitude dry my tears.

The water that once claimed me still calls me.

And every day I whisper back, "Yes, Lord - still."

That is the truest lifestyle-baptism I know: not another ceremony, but a life that keeps agreeing with the one already entered.

Scripture Index

- 1 Corinthians 15:31
- Luke 11:4
- John 20:23
- Romans 6:3–5
- Ephesians 5:25–27
- John 13:10
- Lamentations 3:22–23
- Hebrews 4:12
- Hebrews 10:22

Chapter Twenty-One

No Shame in the Water

The Sound of Chains Hitting Water

Shame has a sound. You can hear it when someone hesitates before walking to the altar, when they linger at the edge of the tank, wondering if God really meant *them*.

But I've also heard another sound - the splash that follows surrender. It's the sound of chains hitting water. And when that happens, even angels lean in to listen.

"There is therefore now no condemnation to them which are in Christ Jesus." (Romans 8:1)

Baptism is heaven's way of shouting that verse back at your past.

Not because water invents the verdict, but because water is allowed to witness it.

Shame Is a Terrible Swimmer

Shame is not silenced by water alone, but by a verdict that water is allowed to witness. Scripture says there are *"three that bear witness on earth: the Spirit, the water, and the Blood"* (1 John 5:8).

The Blood does not argue - it establishes. It declares guilt answered and conscience cleansed. The Water does not decide [62] -

---

[62] See Appendix B - Water Remembers

it testifies that a crossing has taken place, that what was bound has been left behind. And the Spirit does not perform - He bears witness within the heart to what God has already spoken.[63]

Shame cannot survive that agreement. It has no standing where the Blood has answered, no claim where the Water has testified, and no voice where the Spirit confirms sonship. Shame sinks not because it was forgotten, but because heaven rendered a verdict it cannot overturn.

Shame doesn't drown easily - but it can't tread water forever. It gasps for breath in the river of forgiveness. It sinks under the weight of truth.

The problem with shame is that it doesn't just condemn what you've done - it tries to convince you that *you are* what you've done.

That's why baptism is so powerful: it separates who you *were* from who you *are*.

Shame dies because the old self dies; baptism buries what once accused you (Romans 6:4). You don't negotiate with shame - you drown it.

---

[63]In Scripture, guilt is cleansed by blood (Hebrews 9:14), while shame is addressed through vindication and restored standing before God (Isaiah 54:4; Romans 8:1). Baptism does not remove shame mechanically, but bears witness to the verdict that renders shame powerless.

Leaving Babylon Behind

In *Escape the Shame of Babylon*, David Webb wrote that "shame is the internal echo of captivity - a prison that speaks." (32) Baptism silences that echo. It's not just washing; it's walking out.

The Israelites crossed the Red Sea leaving Egypt's whips behind. You cross baptism's waters leaving Babylon's lies behind.

"The Lord has rolled away the reproach of Egypt from you." (Joshua 5:9)

The first baptism of Israel wasn't in a tank - it was in a sea of separation. That same principle still works: what once defined you can't follow you through the flood.

The water does not pretend the old bondage never existed. It simply refuses to let it keep naming you.

Shame's Favorite Lie

Shame whispers,

"If people really knew who you were, they'd never love you."

But baptism shouts,

"The One who really knows you already called you His."

Shame hides; truth reveals - not to humiliate, but to heal. Jesus doesn't drag your sin into the water to embarrass you; He buries it so deep it can't find its way back.

"As far as the east is from the west, so far hath He removed our transgressions from us." (Psalm 103:12)

That is why shame hates the river. The river keeps agreeing with mercy.

The Water Doesn't Blush

People blush. Religion blushes. The water never does.

It has seen everything: saints, sinners, skeptics, prodigals. It has never once refused a soul. The same water that receives a prodigal can receive a preacher.

When you go down, the water doesn't flinch. It doesn't judge. It just does what it's done since Eden - obey.

The water's not embarrassed by your past. It's excited about your future. It does not flatter your sin. It simply does not recoil from your surrender.

The Mirror of Mercy

Baptism is a mirror that tells the truth gently. You see yourself - but you also see who God says you are. It's not just a reflection; it's revelation.

When you rise from the water, you're not carrying your old label anymore. The old names begin to lose their hold. What shame used as a sentence, grace begins to answer with calling.

The water does not invent your new name; it bears witness to the one heaven already knows.

Mercy does not lie to you in that mirror. It tells the truth so clearly that the lie finally has nowhere left to hide.

The Holy Towel Exchange

After one baptism service, a woman told me,

"Pastor, I feel lighter - but I think I left my towel."

I laughed and said, "That's fine. The water lifted what weighed you down; you can leave the towel too."

Sometimes humor and holiness meet in the same sentence. You walk in dripping from shame, and walk out realizing God wasn't holding a grudge - He was holding a towel.

That may be one of mercy's sweetest surprises: the God you expected to shame you is the One who helps dry your face.

The Great Unblushing God

God isn't embarrassed by you. He's not tiptoeing around your past. He rejoices over you with gladness. He has already gone before you to usher you into the Kingdom-Life. He has prepared the way into the promises, plans, purpose, and good works He has established for you in Christ.

"For your shame ye shall have double; and for confusion they shall rejoice in their portion." (Isaiah 61:7)

That's what happens when you come through the water - you trade embarrassment for inheritance. Heaven turns your wounds into weapons, your story into song.

And suddenly, the water you once feared becomes your freedom. The same river you once avoided becomes the place where shame loses jurisdiction.

When the River is Unobstructed

The river has never stopped flowing from the throne of God. What changes is whether it is permitted to flow through us.

Shame does not dry up the river - it dams the heart.

Ezekiel once saw that river flowing from the threshold of the temple. At first it was ankle-deep, then knee-deep, then waist-deep, until finally he said,

"It was a river that I could not pass over, waters to swim in." (Ezekiel 47:5)

The source did not change. The depth changed where it was entered.

Jesus echoed the same truth when He said, *"Out of his belly shall flow rivers of living water"* (John 7:38). The issue was never whether the river existed, but whether the inner man was open enough to release it.

Shame constricts that flow. It teaches the heart to hide, to close, to protect what God intended to pour through. But when shame is answered - not ignored, not suppressed, but answered by repentance, obedience, and truth - the obstruction is removed.

The river does not begin again. It is released again.

And as the blockage gives way, the flow deepens - not because God gives more, but because we finally allow more of Him to pass through us

That's what freedom feels like - when you stop wading and start swimming. When you stop managing grace and start moving with it. [64]

What began as a trickle through the temple of your heart becomes a torrent. The shame that once blocked the flow has now broken open.

The same presence that flowed from Eden still flows through you - *"And a river went out of Eden to water the garden."* (Genesis 2:10)

And in the last book of Scripture, that river returns - *"And he showed me a pure river of water of life, clear as crystal, proceeding out of the throne of God and of the Lamb."* (Revelation 22:1)

From Eden to Ezekiel, from Jesus to you, the story never changed - God has always been a River looking for a willing channel.

Once the shame is gone, the flow comes back.

You were never meant to live as a reservoir of regret, but as a river of renewal. That's the miracle of baptism - not just what goes down, but what comes back up and starts to flow.

---

[64] See Appendix A: Word Study Spotlight – CHARIS (grace)

Reflection – The Water Remembers

The water doesn't blush. It doesn't recoil. It remembers obedience, not offense.

Every soul that enters adds one more echo of grace.

The river has seen worse than you and loved every story it carried away.

So when shame whispers from the shore, just smile and wave.

The water knows your real name. And heaven has already declared it over you.

Scripture Index

- Ezekiel 47:5
- Genesis 2:10
- Isaiah 61:7
- John 7:38
- Joshua 5:9
- Psalm 103:12
- Revelation 22:1
- Romans 6:4
- Romans 8:1
- 1 John 5:8

Part Five

Joy in the Journey

If heaven rejoices over one sinner who repents, you can bet joy is not absent when one of them cannonballs into the baptistry.

Chapter Twenty-Two

Stories from the Water

The Holy Splash Zone

Baptism is sacred - but sometimes it's hilarious. For every tear shed in the water, there is often a moment no one planned: a nervous laugh, a sudden splash, an unexpected stumble. And somehow, those moments don't cheapen the holy - they individualize it.

And maybe that's the point. God made water. He made laughter. He does not seem nearly as nervous about the collision as religious people do.

"A merry heart doeth good like a medicine." (Proverbs 17:22)

I've watched enough baptisms to know: the water's holy, but it has never required everyone to keep a straight face.

The sacred is not sterile. Sometimes it arrives with tears. Sometimes with trembling. Sometimes with a splash no one saw coming.

Leading People to the Water (Without Chasing Them Downstream)

I tell people all the time,

"If you force me to baptize you in the river, you better be ready to meet God - because if I lose you, I'm not coming in after you. I can't swim."

Faith does not require foolishness. Some of us are called to lead people to the water, not chase them downstream. Wisdom and obedience are not enemies- especially in hip-waders.

The river is holy. It is not impressed by our recklessness.

Hip Waders and Humility

Once I borrowed a pair of hip waders from a pastor friend built like Samson after leg day. Those waders were so large I could have smuggled an usher in each leg.

The man I was baptizing towered over me, broad-shouldered and nervous. I whispered, "It's fine, brother - just lean back." He did. Too far.

The waders filled instantly. I started sinking while trying to lift him. He came up shouting; I came up sputtering. The congregation thought it was revival. I thought it was my obituary.

Humility comes fast when your waterproof gear turns into a personal aquarium. The water has a way of reminding us - no one leaves unchanged.

The Drumstick Incident

Another time, I was on the praise team during baptisms. Right as one man went under, the drummer lost his stick. It shot across the platform like a holy javelin, missed the minister's ear by an inch, and landed on the edge of the tank - teetering like judgment day. I grabbed it before it fell, handed it back, and we kept singing.

That's what I call cooperation between the body of Christ - one plays, one dunks, one catches. All things done decently and in order… mostly.

When Legalism Learns to Swim

Then there are the well-meaning legalists. You know the ones - terrified someone's feet didn't go all the way under.

I knew a minister once who baptized a man who panicked halfway down. As the man went under, he reached up to grab the edge of the tank. His hand missed, and his feet went up in the air out of the water. The minister, bless his heart, shoved the feet into the water so his whole body was submerged - just in case those unbaptized feet decided to rebel later.

He told me afterward, "I realized how silly it was - as if those feet were going to start sinning on their own."

We laughed. But the truth behind the joke is sobering: When we make baptism about performance instead of posture, we miss the purpose entirely.

God isn't measuring submersion by the inch; He's measuring surrender by the intent of the heart.

The river was never meant to become a measuring tape.

Cannonballs and the Kingdom

Somewhere online, there's a kid who, when asked to step into the baptistry, did a full cannonball instead. Water everywhere. Choir soaked. Sanctuary gasped. Joy won the room.

I don't know that boy's name, but I'm convinced his theology was sound:

"If you're going under, go all in."

Maybe baptism should look like that more often - reckless joy, total commitment, no hesitation. Faith that jumps instead of tiptoes.

Not irreverence. Full surrender with both feet off the ground.

The Pastor Who Slipped

A minister lowering a man in a portable tank. Everything looks smooth - until the preacher's foot slips. Both vanish under the water like synchronized swimmers. When they came up, soaked head-to-toe, the minister just grinned and shouted,

"We both needed it!"

Sometimes the baptizer gets baptized too.

The Gospel According to the Horse Trough

Over the years, I've learned that the water goes where the willing are. I've helped drag tanks into nursing-home courtyards, baptized people in their bathtubs, and watched others go down in the bucket of a backhoe. Once, we even carried a woman from her wheelchair into a baptistry so she could rise again with dignity and joy.

Every situation is different, and that's the beauty of it - the gospel meets people where they are, not where it's convenient.

When my son decided to be baptized, he wanted to wear swim goggles, nose plugs, and ear plugs. He has sensory sensitivities - he doesn't like sand on his feet or water in his ears. We worked with that, because baptism isn't about enduring discomfort; it's about expressing devotion. The same water that met John in the Jordan will meet a child in swim gear just as gladly.

But the day that still makes me laugh happened at a soul-winning block party in a major city. We were baptizing people in an eight-foot horse trough set on a trailer. One man who stepped forward was… let's just say, *built for buoyancy.*

I helped him climb onto the trailer while four other men gathered around to assist. He sat on the edge of the tank, and we guided one leg, then the other, into the water. I said, "Alright, now just slide forward and we'll help you down."

Here's what I forgot: buoyancy. Fat floats.

The moment he slid forward, he popped up like a human life preserver. We all looked at each other for a split second, then someone said, "Grab a limb!" Five ministers, each holding an arm or a leg, one with a hand on his shoulder - and together we performed what can only be described as a synchronized dunk.

That's when I remembered the *other* law of water: displacement. When he went under, the horse trough turned into the Red Sea. A tidal wave rolled off the trailer, drenching all five of us head-to-toe.

We didn't laugh right away - we were too stunned and half-blind from the splash. But later, when we regrouped, the laughter came in waves too. Because if heaven rejoices over one sinner who repents, I have no doubt joy was present that day too.

The point isn't how much water we used - it's that love made room for a man who wanted to belong. And if five soaked preachers were the price of one redeemed soul, it was a bargain heaven gladly honored.

Why Laughter Belongs in the Water

We often act like the Holy Spirit is allergic to humor. But joy is heaven's native language. The same Spirit who convicts also comforts - and sometimes, He is not threatened when joy shows up dripping.

Laughter doesn't cheapen baptism; it reminds us we're human. And humanity, redeemed and dripping, is God's favorite miracle.

"The joy of the Lord is your strength." (Nehemiah 8:10)

If joy is strength, then every laugh in the water is the sound of divine favor stretching our hearts.

When my children were born, I was there each time when the water broke. Each moment was different - each child unique - but with every birth, my heart grew larger. I didn't know love could multiply like that. I learned that love is exponential; it expands with every life you touch.

One of my daughters didn't cry when she was born - she came out humming. It startled the doctor, but it made perfect sense to me later. Every soul enters the world with its own song. Some cry, some laugh, some hum their way into life.

Baptism is no different. I've seen people rise from the water shouting, others weeping, others whispering, and one man who came up and said, "Do it again."

That's why we can't turn baptism into a ceremony scripted for spectators. It's not a performance to observe; it's a birth to celebrate.

Some churches want everyone silent and reverent - but the moment isn't about the crowd. It's about the person meeting God in the water.

And our duty, as those who help them, is to meet them *where they are* - to make them feel safe, seen, and surrounded by joy as they're born again into the Kingdom of God.

Every birth looks a little different, but heaven recognizes them all.

The Sacred and the Silly

The baptistry has seen it all - trembling grandmothers, fearless children, prodigals, and professors. It has held tears, laughter, and everything in between.

Sometimes the sacred and the silly collide, and that's where the best stories live.

Because the gospel isn't sterile - it's soaked. It's messy. Joyful. A celebration where mercy and mischief share the same pew.

That is not disrespect. That is incarnation. Holy things keep happening in human moments.

Reflection - Holy Water, Human Moments

Heaven doesn't mind getting splashed. The God who parted seas can handle puddles.

So laugh. Let the joy bubble up like living water.

For every solemn prayer whispered in the tank, there is also room in the Kingdom for joy to answer back.

Because favor isn't fragile - it's fluid.

Scriptural References

- Proverbs 17:22
- Nehemiah 8:10
- Luke 15:7
- Philippians 4:4
- John 3:3–5

Chapter Twenty-Three

Why Did I Get Wet?

One River, A Lifelong Yes

What began in the water as a boy did not end there.

I was young, cold, and certain of only one thing: God was real, and I wanted to belong to Him. I could not have explained covenant that day. I could not have mapped blood, water, and Spirit with any precision. I only knew that heaven was dealing with me, and I wanted to answer.

That moment marked me. It began a lifelong conversation between heaven and water.

Later seasons taught me what that first surrender actually meant. Ministry taught me how easy it is to trade presence for productivity. Sorrow taught me how quickly a human heart can grow heavy. Loss taught me that even people who love God can start walking like they have forgotten the sound of the river. But what the water witnessed over me in that first obedience kept speaking. It would not let me settle for noise when God was calling for surrender.

My story with the water did not end in childhood. But the deepest truth in it was never the number of times I stood near it. The deepest truth was that what God had declared there kept reaching deeper than I first understood.

The Answer of a Good Conscience

Peter said it this way:

"Baptism now saves you - not the removal of dirt from the body, but the answer of a good conscience toward God." (1 Peter 3:21)

That line has stayed with me for years. Baptism is not magic water. It is not a religious trick. It is not a way of buying what only Christ could secure. It is an answer - embodied, open, unmistakable. A conscience no longer hiding. A life no longer arguing. A heart saying yes where it once stalled.

That is why baptism stays with you. The act happens in time, but its witness keeps unfolding. It keeps asking whether your life still agrees with what your body once declared in the water.

Covenant in the Water

The covenant was not sealed in water. It was sealed in blood.

That matters.

The cross established what the river never could. The Blood spoke where guilt had been shouting. The Lamb secured what no human obedience could ever negotiate. But once heaven had established covenant in Christ, the water was appointed to bear witness to it in the earth.

That is why baptism matters so much in this book. Not because it replaces the cross, and not because it competes with grace, but because covenant love asks for embodied response. God did not save us into abstraction. He did not leave surrender trapped in the invisible. He gave it a witness.

The Blood establishes. The water bears witness. The Spirit confirms.

And when those witnesses agree, a life is no longer merely thinking about God. It is stepping openly into what God has made possible.

Birth Brought Into View

Baptism is also birth brought into view.

The Father draws. The Word conceives. The Blood secures. The Spirit breathes. And the water stands there as witness that what heaven began is now pressing into open life.

That is why Jesus spoke to Nicodemus the way He did. New birth was never meant to remain a private idea, admired from a distance like a doctrine in a notebook. God brings forth what He conceives. He does not plant life just to leave it hidden forever.

So when I think back to that first baptism, I no longer see only a nervous boy in cold water. I see a beginning brought into view. I see heaven letting earth witness what it had already begun inside me. I see birth stepping out of abstraction and into embodied obedience.

I did not understand all of that then. But heaven was not waiting on my vocabulary.

The Weight That Floats Away

There is another reason the water keeps speaking long after the clothes dry: it teaches you what to lay down.

Not just sin in the broad sense, though God knows the cross dealt with that. I mean sediment. The residue of self-effort. The film of disappointment. The grit of pride, fear, grief, performance, and old noise that settles on a human walk.

Baptism has a way of telling the truth about weight.

When you come up, what remains is often not excitement, but lightness. Peace. Perspective. Sometimes tears. Sometimes laughter. Sometimes the kind of stillness that feels stronger than shouting.

Freedom does not always sound dramatic. Sometimes it sounds like breath returning.

The Water's Witness

I did not write this book to make people fascinated with water. I wrote it because Scripture refuses to treat water like scenery.

From Genesis, God keeps meeting people there. He hovers over it. He parts it. He appoints it. He fills it with witness. He receives His Son in it. He commands disciples to use it. And Scripture finally says out loud what the whole book has been whispering all along:

 (1 John 5:8)

That is the center of it for me now.

The water is not random. The cross is not abstract. The Spirit is not silent.

Heaven keeps pursuing what it loves, and baptism stands in the earth as one of the places where that pursuit becomes visible.

Why Did I Get Wet?

Because God was not done speaking.

Because obedience is still the language of love.

Because covenant is too real to leave trapped inside private intention.

Because new birth is too alive to remain invisible.

Because sometimes your next step forward starts with going under.

I got wet because Christ had opened covenant, and I wanted my body to agree with what heaven was saying. I got wet because I wanted to belong to the God who had already begun dealing with me. I got wet because the Father draws, and drawn people eventually have to answer.

I got wet because the cross dealt with my sin, but the water taught my whole person what surrender looks like.

And maybe that is why you have stayed with this book. Because something in you knows there is more than one way to stand dry on a shore. Some people stand there in fear. Some in tradition. Some in confusion. Some in delay dressed up as discernment.

But eventually the Spirit still says what He has always said: Come.

And when He does, the question is not whether the river is ready.

The question is whether you are done calling hesitation wisdom.

Reflection - The Final Ripple

The river still runs. The Spirit still hovers. The Blood still speaks. And the invitation still stands.

Why did I get wet?

Because heaven revealed, covenant had opened, new life was pressing toward birth, and obedience required a body.

That is still my answer.

And if the Witnesses agree, it is enough.

One-sentence summary

Baptism is the embodied yes to the risen Jesus - covenant witnessed in water, new birth brought into view, and surrender established on earth as the Spirit, the water, and the Blood agree.

Scriptural References

- 1 John 5:8
- John 3:5
- Romans 6:4
- Acts 19:1–6
- Philippians 3:13–14
- 1 Peter 3:21

Conclusion

The Conclusion of the Whole Matter

Baptism isn't a spell, and it isn't a stage. It's obedience answering a covenant already established. The blood of Jesus established the covenant (Matthew 26:28; Hebrews 9:22). The water bears witness on earth that you've crossed from the old life into the new (Romans 6:3–4; 1 John 5:8). And the Spirit seals what God has begun, His own mark and earnest of inheritance (Ephesians 1:13–14).

The blood establishes.

The water bears witness.

The Spirit seals.

That is the whole matter.

So if the river is calling, do not waste your life arguing with the shoreline. Step in. Let the witnesses agree.

Appendix A

Word Study Spotlight: CHARIS

"Charis Isn't Pixie Dust"

Somewhere between the upper room and your favorite study Bible, *grace* got strange. People started treating it like spiritual electricity - invisible power surging through your soul so you can do what you couldn't. That's poetic, maybe even comforting, but it's not Greek. Not the way the apostles used it. And definitely not the way Jesus lived it.

What the Word Really Means

The word translated *grace* in your New Testament is χάρις (charis). Before anyone ever wrote a Gospel, *charis* meant one thing in Greek culture:

"A pleasant disposition of favor or goodwill from a giver toward someone they delight in."

In plain English: *charis* isn't power. It's posture. It's not a magic energy; it's a smile in the heart of the giver.

If you had *charis* toward your neighbor, it meant you *liked* them enough to do something kind - not because they earned it, but because you wanted to. The act that followed (the gift, the help, the rescue) wasn't *charis* itself; it was what *charis* produced.

When Scripture says, *"Noah found grace in the eyes of the Lord"* (Genesis 6:8), the Hebrew word is *ḥēn* - favor, gracious regard, divine delight. When the ancient translators rendered this passage into Greek, they chose the word *charis*, the same word the New Testament uses for God's gracious disposition toward His people.

Noah did not earn rescue; he received favor. God's gracious posture toward him - His *ḥēn*, His *charis* - moved Him to act. The deliverance was the result of grace, not the definition of it."

Charis in the New Testament

When the apostles wrote of the *charis* of God, they weren't describing mystical energy flowing through your veins. They were describing the favoring disposition of God revealed in Christ, not a blanket approval of all men in all conditions, but His holy kindness that calls men towards Him and rests upon those who yield. The divine smile that moves Him to act on our behalf.

That's why Luke can write,

"The child grew and became strong in spirit... and the *charis* of God was upon Him." (Luke 2:40) Jesus didn't need forgiveness or extra power. He lived under the open smile of His Father.

Paul used *charis* the same way - as shorthand for *God's favor at work.* When he said, *"By charis you have been saved"* (Ephesians 2:8), he wasn't saying, "You're saved by cosmic electricity." He was saying, "You're saved because God wanted you - and He acted on that desire."

Grace is not God approving everyone equally; it is God leaning mercifully toward the undeserving, and being received most fully by those who humble themselves and align with Him.

So, What Happened?

Centuries later, as Greek became Latin and theology went Roman, *charis* got promoted from a divine smile to a divine substance - something God injected into the soul to make you holy. That wasn't Bible Greek; that was *gratia infusa* - philosophy in priestly robes.

The result? We started teaching that grace was a "thing" you could run out of, grow in, or borrow. But in the original language, *charis* isn't a thing at all. It's the attitude of the Giver. And good news - His attitude doesn't fluctuate.

Charis vs. Forgiveness

Let's make it plain: Grace is not forgiveness. Different word. Different world.

- Forgiveness = ἄφεσις (*aphesis*) - the release or letting go.
- Grace = χάρις (*charis*) - the favor that decides to release.

One cancels the debt; the other smiles while doing it. One is legal; the other is relational.

Forgiveness is the act. Grace is the attitude that caused it.

Kirkland's Translation

If I were translating *charis* for this in scripture and daily life, I'd write it like this:

"God's delighted favor - His willingness to lean toward you and do good because He wants to."

That's *charis*.

Not lightning.

Not leniency.

Not license.

It's the kindness of a Father whose heart tilts toward His children - and because His heart leans, His hand moves.

Reflection

Grace isn't a river flowing through you; it's a smile flowing from Him.

It doesn't buzz or sparkle. It simply *is* - His permanent posture of favor.

Forgiveness cleans the page. *Charis* writes the story.

Final Word

If you've ever been told grace is "God's power working through you," smile and nod - then remember this: Power is what God *does*. Grace is how God *feels* when He does it.

For the Study-Minded

Before we go any further, we need our words to stay in their lanes. Charis is favor - God's initiative moving toward you. Eleos is mercy - compassion that withholds what you deserve and stoops to help. Aphesis is release - remission that lets the prisoner go and sends the debt away. The table isn't here to impress anyone with Greek; it's here to keep us from smuggling modern assumptions into biblical language. When you can see the difference, you can hear the gospel more clearly - favor that draws, mercy that meets, and release that frees.

Greek Term	Transliteration	Meaning	Function
χάρις	*charis*	Favor, goodwill, gracious attitude	The giver's disposition
ἄφεσις	*aphesis*	Release, pardon	Forgiveness of sins
ἔλεος	*eleos*	Mercy, compassion	Withholding deserved penalty

65

References

Bauer, W., Danker, F. W., Arndt, W. F., & Gingrich, F. W. (2000). *A Greek-English lexicon of the New Testament and other early Christian literature* (3rd ed.). University of Chicago Press.

Louw, J. P., & Nida, E. A. (1989). *Greek-English lexicon of the New Testament: Based on semantic domains* (2nd ed., Vols. 1–2). United Bible Societies.

Silva, M. (Ed.). (2014). *New international dictionary of New Testament theology and exegesis* (2nd ed.). Zondervan.

Mounce, W. D. (2006). *Mounce's complete expository dictionary of Old and New Testament words*. Zondervan.

---

[65] Definitions summarized from standard NT Greek lexicons; see BDAG, s.v. χάρις, ἔλεος, ἄφεσις; and Louw & Nida (semantic domains) for usage ranges.

Appendix B

Water Remembers - The Oldest Witness in Creation

Before a prophet ever thundered, before Adam ever stood upright, before sin ever cast its first shadow - water was there.

Before covenant. Before sacrifice. Before the Word (logos) became flesh - the Spirit hovered over the waters (Genesis 1:2), and creation's oldest witness listened for God's voice.

Water was the first congregation beneath the first sermon. It was the first altar under the breath of God. So when we talk about baptismal waters today, do not imagine cheap tap water with nothing to say. Water has a history. Water has a testimony. Water remembers God.

Water Responds When God Draws Near

"The voice of the LORD is over the waters…" (Psalm 29:3)

Water does not think as men think - but Scripture insists it responds.

When God speaks, water reacts. When God approaches, water trembles. When God commands, water obeys.

"The waters saw You, O God; the waters saw You and were afraid; the depths also trembled." (Psalm 77:16)

This is not myth. It is the Bible's own poetry of witness.

Water recognizes the presence of God not with intellect, but with obedience, not with consciousness, but with resonance.

Deep reacts to Depth.

Water Calls and Water Answers

"Deep calls unto deep at the sound of Your waterfalls…" (Psalm 42:7)

Everywhere in Scripture, water is portrayed as responsive, never passive, never indifferent.

When God moves, water moves. When God speaks, water echoes. When God reveals Himself, water reacts.

Water is creation's first choir - and it still sings.

Water Remembers the Moments God Passed Through

It remembered the terror of judgment in Noah's day. It remembered the parting of the sea when Israel walked free. It remembered the Jordan folding back for Joshua's priests. It remembered Elijah's mantle striking the river in obedience. It remembered the Lamb of God descending into its depths… and the heavens tearing open above Him.

"The waters saw You…" (Psalm 77:16). They recognized Him every time.

That is memory - not cognitive, but covenantal. Not intellectual, but responsive. Not mystical, but biblical.

Water Obeys Instantly

"Even the wind and the sea obey Him." (Mark 4:41)

Creation doesn't negotiate with divinity. The sea did not need a theology lesson. It simply understood His authority.

Water is the one element in Scripture that never argues with God.

- It parts.

- It rises.

- It stills.

- It flows.

Because water has always known the sound of the Creator's voice.

Water Testifies - It Is a Legal Witness

"There are three that bear witness on the earth: the Spirit, the water, and the blood..." (1 John 5:8)

A witness does one thing - it tells the truth.

Water cannot think, but water can testify. It holds the memory of God's movements, it participates in His miracles, and it aligns with His covenant.

Water keeps the record. Water remembers the covenant. Water tells the truth of what God has done.

That is why baptism matters -not because water saves, but because water agrees with what salvation declares.

Creation Itself Remembers God's Movements

"All the ends of the earth shall remember and turn to the LORD…" (Psalm 22:27)

If the *earth* remembers, how much more the waters that first heard His voice?

Creation does not forget revelation. It resonates with it. Water, especially so.

This is why baptism is not symbolic alone - it is participatory. You step into the same element that witnessed creation, judgment, deliverance, and resurrection.

So What Happens When You Enter the Water?

When you step into baptismal waters, you enter something ancient, something obedient, something that has been waiting for you since Genesis.

You are not stepping into *new* water. You are stepping into remembering water - water that has already obeyed Moses, already carried Elijah, already opened for Joshua, already embraced Jesus.

Water testifies again when you step in:

- to the death it remembers from the Flood and the Cross,
- to the deliverance it remembers from the Red Sea and Resurrection morning,
- to the life it remembers from creation itself.

Your baptism becomes part of water's long witness.

Final Reflection - What Water Remembers About You

If water remembers God's voice, it remembers your surrender. If water trembles at His presence, it rejoices at your repentance. If water obeyed Him through every covenant, it gladly participates in yours.

Water does not change its testimony - but when you rise from burial to breath, you change your identity within its story.

Because baptism is not merely your act of obedience - it is creation agreeing that the One who began His story in water has begun His story in you.

Appendix C

The Witness of the Blood

What Scripture Actually Says the Blood Does

The Bible never treats blood as magical, mystical, or autonomous. But it also never treats it as incidental.

From Genesis to Revelation, blood is not a personality - it is a God-appointed covenant medium. Scripture does not give blood independent agency, but it *does* assign it real, legally recognized function within God's covenant order.

To understand baptism, forgiveness, and conscience cleansing rightly, we must understand what the blood witnesses - and what it does not.

The Life Is in the Blood (Not the Power)

Scripture is explicit:

"For the life of the flesh is in the blood, and I have given it to you upon the altar to make atonement for your souls." (Leviticus 17:11)

Blood does not possess power of its own. It carries life, and God assigns it covenant purpose.

The authority of blood is not intrinsic - it is delegated. God says, *"I have given it to you…"*

Blood functions because God honors what He appoints, not because blood acts independently.

Blood Establishes Covenant - It Does Not Negotiate It

Every biblical covenant that dealt with sin, access, or inheritance involved blood:

- Circumcision (Genesis 17)
- Passover (Exodus 12)
- Sinai sacrifices (Exodus 24)
- Day of Atonement (Leviticus 16)
- The Cross (Matthew 26:28)

Blood does not decide terms. It ratifies what God has already spoken.

"For where there is a covenant, there must also be the death of the one who made it." (Hebrews 9:16)

In Scripture, blood is the legal seal, not the author.

Blood Cleanses the Conscience - Not the Body

The Old Testament is clear that animal blood never perfected anyone internally:

"It is not possible that the blood of bulls and goats could take away sins." (Hebrews 10:4)

What changed at the Cross was not blood itself, but whose blood was shed.

"How much more shall the blood of Christ... cleanse your conscience from dead works to serve the living God?" (Hebrews 9:14)

This is critical:

- Water cleanses the **body**

- Blood cleanses the **conscience**

- The Spirit transforms the **inner life**

No witness replaces the others. They function together - but distinctly.

"The Blood Speaks" - What Scripture Actually Means

Scripture does say:

"The blood of sprinkling speaks better things than that of Abel." (Hebrews 12:24)

This is legal language reminder, not personification.

Abel's blood *"cried out"* for justice (Genesis 4:10). Christ's blood testifies to fulfilled justice and mercy.

The blood does not argue. The blood does not decide. The blood does not initiate.

It testifies that the price has been paid.

The Blood as Witness (1 John 5:6–8)

John writes:

"There are three that bear witness on earth: the Spirit, the water, and the blood; and these three agree."

Agreement matters.

- The Blood testifies that the covenant has been ratified.

- The Water testifies that a person has submitted to that covenant.

- The Spirit testifies that the life of God is now present.

The blood does not override repentance. The water does not replace the cross. The Spirit does not ignore obedience.

They agree - they do not compete.

Why the Blood Had to Come Before Christian Baptism

John's baptism could prepare hearts, but it could not remove guilt:

"Without the shedding of blood there is no remission." (Hebrews 9:22)

That is why baptism changes after the Cross.

Before Calvary:

- Water prepared
- Repentance awakened
- Remission awaited

After Calvary:

- Blood secures remission
- Water bears witness to a finished work
- The Spirit indwells what has been cleansed

The blood did not make water powerful. It made water authorized.

The Blood Does Not Replace Obedience

The New Testament never uses the blood to excuse disobedience.

"You were redeemed… with the precious blood of Christ." (1 Peter 1:18–19)

Redemption is not exemption. The blood opens the door - it does not eliminate the path.

Grace does not act. Blood does not act. God acts - and blood witnesses to what He has done.

What the Blood Does *Not* Do

For clarity, Scripture never teaches that the blood:

- Acts independently
- Saves without faith
- Overrides repentance
- Negates obedience
- Replaces baptism
- Functions as a formula

The blood is not a mechanism. It is a witness to covenant fulfillment.

Summary: The Proper Place of the Blood

The blood is not mystical. The blood is not autonomous. The blood is not optional.

It is God's appointed witness that the covenant has been ratified, conscience has been cleansed, and access has been opened.

The blood does not compete with water or Spirit. It agrees with them.

And when all three witnesses stand together, heaven recognizes the testimony.

The blood does not shout. It does not argue. It simply stands in agreement with what God has already declared finished.

Appendix D

The Witness of the Spirit

Breath, Wind, and the Life God Animates

The Holy Spirit is not an impersonal emotion, nor an independent agent acting apart from God's will. Scripture consistently presents the Spirit as God's own breath and wind - proceeding from Him, directed by Him, and testifying to what He has already established.

The Greek word translated *Spirit* is pneuma, meaning *breath, wind, or moving air.* The Hebrew equivalent, *ruach*, carries the same meaning.

This matters.

Because breath has force, but not autonomy. Wind has movement, but not intent of its own. Breath animates life - but only as the giver directs it.

The Spirit as Breath from the Beginning

The first time the Spirit appears in Scripture, it is not speaking, but as the movement of God's breath.

"The Spirit (ruach) of God moved upon the face of the waters." (Genesis 1:2)

Creation did not begin with argument, emotion, or ritual. It began when God breathed movement into what He had already spoken.

Later, when God formed man:

"The LORD God breathed into his nostrils the breath (neshamah) of life; and man became a living soul." (Genesis 2:7)

The breath did not decide to give life. The breath carried the intention of the One who breathed.

Life began when God directed His breath into formed dust.

This establishes the pattern Scripture never abandons:

- God speaks
- God breathes
- Life responds

Pneuma Does Not Act Alone - It Proceeds

Jesus reinforced this same understanding:

"The wind (pneuma) blows where it wishes, and you hear the sound of it, but cannot tell where it comes from or where it goes." (John 3:8)

Jesus did not say the wind decides. He said it moves, and its presence is known by its effect.

Wind is identified not by intention, but by response.

So it is with the Spirit.

Jesus and the Directed Breath

After the resurrection, Scripture records something precise and intentional:

"He breathed on them and said, 'Receive the Holy Spirit.'" (John 20:22)

This was not symbolism. This was Genesis replayed.

- God breathed → Adam lived
- Jesus breathed → disciples received life for mission -a foreshadowing of what was to come.

The breath did not choose recipients. Jesus directed it.

The Spirit did not initiate the moment. Christ authorized it.

Pentecost: Wind Before Fire

At Pentecost, the Spirit did not arrive as a personality making introductions.

He arrived as wind:

"There came a sound from heaven as of a rushing mighty wind." (Acts 2:2)

Before tongues of fire appeared, before speech erupted, before power was manifested,

Breath filled the house.

The wind did not preach. The wind did not command. The wind filled space, and people responded.

Fire followed readiness. Wind preceded empowerment.

What the Spirit Does - As Breath

Breath does three things consistently in Scripture:

1. **Animates** what already exists

2. **Moves** what has been aligned

3. **Sustains** what has been born

Breath does not:

- Decide covenant

- Negotiate forgiveness

- Override the will

- Replace obedience

The Spirit gives motion to what heaven has authorized.

That is why Scripture says:

"The Spirit bears witness…" (Romans 8:16)

Witness - not verdict. Confirmation - not initiation.

Why the Spirit Does Not Replace Water or Blood

Breath does not conceive life - seed does. Breath does not deliver birth - water does. Breath does not ratify covenant - blood does.

Breath animates life once it exists.

This is why Scripture never allows the Spirit to bypass:

- Repentance

- Blood

- Baptism

The Spirit fills vessels - He does not form them.

Sealing Revisited: Breath Inside What Belongs to God

When Scripture says believers are *"sealed"* by the Spirit (Ephesians 1:13), it does not mean emotionally secured or spiritually finished.

A seal in Scripture means ownership and presence.

The Spirit's indwelling breath says:

"This life now belongs to God."

It does not say:

"This life no longer requires obedience."

Breath fills what has been claimed - it does not claim what has not been surrendered.

Fire as Breath in Action

Fire is not a separate baptism. Fire is what the Spirit's breath does when it finds something already yielded.

In Scripture, fire does not fall on the casual or the careless, it falls where God has been honored, where the offering is set apart, and where obedience has prepared the ground. Elijah rebuilt the altar, set the sacrifice in order, and then called on the Lord, and the fire of the Lord fell (1 Kings 18:30–39). At the tabernacle and the temple, glory filled the house, and fire came as God marked what He had claimed (Exodus 40:34–35; 2 Chronicles 7:1–

3). At Pentecost, the disciples were together in obedience, waiting under instruction, and then tongues like fire rested upon them (Acts 2:1–4).

That pattern holds: washing and consecration before approach (Numbers 19; Exodus 30:17–21), surrender before service (Romans 12:1), and then fire, not to destroy what is His, but to reveal it. God is a consuming fire (Hebrews 12:29), and what He consumes first is not people, it is competition. Fire does not "pick victims." Fire manifests where a life has been placed on the altar and kept there.

The Spirit Has Power - But Not Autonomy

Scripture never attributes independent decision-making to the Spirit.

Jesus said plainly:

"He will not speak of Himself." (John 16:13)

The Spirit proceeds. The Spirit testifies. The Spirit animates.

All power flows from the One who breathes.

Summary: The Witness of Breath

Where the Blood establishes covenant, and the Water witnesses surrender, the Spirit breathes life into what God has claimed.

The Spirit does not act apart from God - It is God's breath in motion.

And wherever that breath moves, life responds.

The Spirit is not the author of covenant - It is the breath that makes covenant life move.

Before

Appendix E

Roasting Cows

(With the Goal of Peace, Not Division)

A Necessary Disclaimer Before We Light the Grill

Before we roast anything, let's say this plainly:

This appendix is not written to divide the Church, discredit sincere believers, or label anyone a heretic. Many of the traditions addressed here were embraced honestly, taught faithfully, and practiced with genuine devotion to God. They did not invalidate our walk with Him. They did not nullify our prayers, our growth, or His work in our lives.

God is gracious. He meets people in partial understanding all the time.

But Scripture also shows us something else: there comes a moment when greater clarity invites deeper alignment.

Apollos was "mighty in the Scriptures" and fervent in spirit - yet still needed Aquila and Priscilla to explain the way of God more accurately. That moment did not shame him; it strengthened him. He was not rejected - he was refined.

This appendix exists for that reason.

Not to mock traditions, but to examine them honestly. Not to burn people, but to remove burdens Scripture never placed.

Not to fracture unity, but to restore harmony between belief and obedience.

Every "cow" addressed here represents a teaching many of us inherited, not invented. Roasting them is not rebellion - it's stewardship. Truth handled humbly does not divide the body; it heals it.

With that said - let's talk about the cows.

The Sacred Cow Roast: Things We Baptized but God Didn't

Before we fire up the grill for our sacred cows, remember this: heaven never told us to defend formulas - heaven told us to follow witnesses. The Blood speaks. The Spirit agrees. The water obeys. Everything else is just religious livestock. Time to light the grill.

1. The "Public Confession" Cow

This cow insists baptism is a public confession of faith. Nice idea. No Scripture.

Confession belongs to your mouth (Romans 10:9–10). Baptism belongs to your body. It's not speech - it's surrender.

You don't get baptized *to perform* your faith; you get baptized *to participate* in divine authority. The audience isn't the crowd; it's the Kingdom.

But even more importantly, the real witnesses of baptism were never the congregation. Scripture tells us who attends every baptism: the water, the Spirit, and the Blood (1 John 5:8). Those are the witnesses that matter. Heaven does not wait for an audience to assemble. It waits for obedience to align. When you go into the water, heaven brings its own courtroom.

That does not mean baptism must be hidden. It means publicity is not its purpose.

2. The "Symbol Only" Cow

This one moos that baptism is "just symbolic." But Scripture never calls it *just* anything. Symbols point to something real; baptism participates in it.

When Peter said, *"Baptism doth also now save us"* (1 Peter 3:21), the word translated "save" was **sōzō** - meaning *to heal, to deliver, to make whole*. Baptism isn't a superstition where you buy your ticket to heaven; it's the appointed witness in which heaven answers what the Blood has accomplished - cleansing the conscience and bringing restoration into view (Acts 22:16). It's not about the afterlife - it's about new life.

And this is where ritualists miss the point. The water does not regenerate by chemistry or sacrament. New life is conceived by the Word (logos), secured by the Blood, and animated by the Spirit. The water does not create that life; it bears witness to it. Without the Blood's testimony, the water would have no covenantal authority. With the Blood's testimony, the water becomes a true witness.

If baptism is reduced to a ticket-to-heaven ritual, the whole point has already been lost. Because baptism isn't about escaping earth; it's about embodying heaven here. It resurrects you into the purpose God gave you to live *on* the earth.

The water doesn't heal by magic - but obedience opens the door for God to act. Baptism stands where every dimension of *sōzō* may be openly witnessed and answered: cleansing, healing, renewal, and restoration.

Baptism is not optional because covenant is not optional. Symbol? Yes. "Just" a symbol? Never.

3. The "One and Done" Cow

When Repetition Is Mistaken for Unbelief

This cow panics anytime rebaptism is mentioned. It insists that if someone goes into the water again, it must mean the first baptism "didn't work."

That assumption sounds spiritual - but it isn't biblical.

Under the Law, washings were repetitive by design. Priests washed every time they ministered (Exodus 30:18–21), and the people washed again and again when purification was required (Leviticus 15; Numbers 19). Repetition didn't cancel the last washing - it reinforced readiness.

Some argue that rebaptism proves a lack of faith, as if returning to obedience somehow invalidates the obedience that came before it. Others go further, claiming a second baptism "crucifies the Lord afresh," or nullifies the first, or proves confusion about being born again. And one argument is repeated often enough to sound convincing: *"You can only be born once. A baby only breaks water once."*

All of these objections confuse birth with washing, and identity with obedience.

Scripture never treats baptism as a fragile moment that must be protected from future obedience. It treats it as a responsive act - one that follows revelation. And revelation does not always arrive all at once.

Scripture is not embarrassed by repeated acts of obedience when God appoints them. Naaman dipped seven times. Priests washed repeatedly. Israel crossed water more than once. Repetition in itself is not unbelief.

The idea that rebaptism "crucifies Christ again" borrows language from Hebrews without respecting its context. Hebrews warns against rejecting Christ after fully knowing Him - not against obeying Christ more deeply as revelation increases. Obedience does not re-crucify Jesus; it honors the cross by aligning with it.

Others argue that rebaptism cancels the first baptism. Scripture never says this. A second act of obedience does not erase the first - just as washing today does not invalidate the bath you took yesterday. A child is born once, yes - but that child is washed many times afterward. And no one argues that a bath denies the birth.

Birth establishes life. Washing may express renewed alignment, cleansing, or readiness in different covenant settings.

Baptism does not lose meaning because obedience repeats. Meaning is lost only when obedience stops responding to revelation.

This is why Acts records people being baptized again - not because the first baptism was false, but because understanding had grown. The disciples in Ephesus were not rebuked; they were completed (Acts 19:1–6). Their second baptism did not negate the first - it honored the truth they had just received.

If revelation grows, response may grow with it. And when heaven calls again, the faithful answer is still "yes."

Repetition is not unbelief. It is humility.

That said, this book is not arguing for routine rebaptism, emotional maintenance baptisms, or returning to the tank for every stumble. The issue is revelation, rupture, and response - not religious repetition for its own sake.

This cow can come off the grill now.

4. The "Denominational Tag" Cow

This cow likes labels. It turns baptism into a membership badge.

But baptism isn't about church logos; it's about Kingdom loyalty. No denomination owns the river. Heaven does not outsource authority to committees or councils. The only "baptismal credential" Scripture ever recognizes is alignment with Christ's commission (Matthew 28:18–20). If the authority comes from Jesus, the baptism is valid - whether it happened in a cathedral, a creek, or a cattle trough.

And the early church had to learn this lesson fast. Paul rebuked the Corinthians because they started baptizing their identity into personalities: "I am of Paul," "I am of Apollos," "I am of Cephas" (1 Corinthians 1:12). Paul's response was blunt: "Is Christ divided?" (1 Corinthians 1:13). In other words, the moment you attach yourself to a camp, you turn covenant into a brand and baptism into a tag.

You can be baptized in a river, a horse trough, or a hotel bathtub. The only name that matters is the one that carries authority.

Heaven is not impressed by branding. The real question is not which camp claimed you, but under whose authority you obeyed.

5. The "Available = Necessity" Cow

Every now and then someone tries to sound spiritual and ends up sounding like a fortune cookie with performance anxiety.

This cow shows up whenever baptism gets measured by access instead of authority - as if plumbing sets doctrine.

Some say it like a proverb: *"If water is handy, you should do it."* Others say it by omission: *"We don't offer it much, because it's not that important."* And still others treat it like an optional upgrade: *"If you feel like you need it, we'll make a way."*

Different tones. Same mistake: availability becomes the deciding factor.

Baptism is not necessary because it's available or convenient. Baptism is necessary because heaven revealed it, the Blood authorized it, the Spirit witnesses to it, and Jesus commanded it.

If necessity rises or falls on convenience, then obedience becomes a matter of geography, plumbing, and church scheduling. But the Kingdom doesn't run on availability - it runs on revelation.

Philip and the eunuch didn't baptize because there was water. There was water because there was revelation. (Acts 8:35–39)

Cornelius wasn't baptized because a bathtub happened to be free. He was baptized because heaven had already fallen on his house. (Acts 10:44–48)

The jailer wasn't baptized at midnight because that was the only appointment left. He was baptized because the Word (logos) had cut him to the heart before dawn. (Acts 16:30–33)

So here's the problem with the "availability" mindset in every direction:

- If we **withhold** baptism because it's inconvenient, we quietly teach that obedience is optional.

- If we **offer** baptism only when people "feel led," we turn a command into a preference.

- If we **preach** baptism only when the setup is easy, we train people to wait for comfort instead of responding to conviction.

Baptism isn't driven by circumstance. It's driven by witness - Water receiving, Spirit descending, Blood declaring (1 John 5:6–8).

The moment you say, "If it's available," you turn a covenant into a convenience and a command into a suggestion. But baptism isn't a suggestion; it's alignment. And alignment doesn't wait for availability - it responds to revelation.

God is not the God of "If it's convenient," He is the God of "This is My beloved Son - hear Him." (Matthew 17:5)

So yes, water matters. But revelation is what makes water meaningful. Necessity flows from obedience, not opportunity.

This cow can stop mooing now.

6. The Age Requirement Cow

Birthday Theology Isn't Bible Theology. Some folks treat baptism like a theme park ride with a "You Must Be This Old To

Enter" sign. Eight years old. Twelve years old. Teenager. Adult. Pick your tradition, pick your number.

But Scripture never ties baptism to age. It ties it to revelation, repentance, and readiness.

God doesn't check your birth certificate; He checks your heart.

From Genesis to Acts, the pattern is the same: Someone hears the Word (logos) - faith ignites - repentance softens - obedience responds. There is no verse that says, "When thy child hath reached the age of accountability, dunk them."

Infants can't repent. Newborns don't experience godly sorrow. Babies don't understand witness, covenant, or resurrection.

Baptism isn't about being old enough; it's about being awake enough.

As Kevin Rice writes in *Cultivating the New Nature*: "God does not wait for perfect maturity; He waits for honest surrender."

Age never disqualified anyone in Scripture. But lack of revelation did. And lack of repentance did. And lack of faith did.

The Kingdom is not chronological; it is covenantal.

7. The Unbaptized Heart Cow

Why Ritual Alone Can't Birth You.

There is a cow that likes to moo loudly in some circles: "If you get the water on a person, the job is done."

As if salvation is a wet version of "tag - you're it."

But without faith, repentance, revelation, and the blood that speaks, baptism is just a bath with better lighting.

Jesus didn't say, *"He that gets wet shall be saved."* He said, *"He that believes AND is baptized…"* (Mark 16:16).

Belief is not optional. Repentance is not optional. The Father drawing is not optional (John 6:44).

And the blood? It is never optional. Without the blood, the water cannot witness (1 John 5:6–8).

Ritual cannot conceive a new nature. Only the Word (logos) can. Water can birth what has been conceived, but it cannot conceive anything by itself.

The heart must awaken before the body gets wet.

8 The Replacement Cow

When People Try to Fire the Water and Hire the Spirit.

A popular modern cow insists that Spirit baptism replaces water baptism. "Once the Spirit has filled you," the cow proclaims, "the water is unnecessary. Outdated. Redundant. Retired."

But Acts never treats the Spirit as a substitute for water. It treats the Spirit as a co-witness with the water under the authority of the Blood.

Cornelius' house received the Spirit first - but Peter still commanded water (Acts 10:44–48). The Samaritans received water first - but needed the Spirit afterward (Acts 8:12–17). Paul had both, quickly and in sequence (Acts 9:17–18).

Water and Spirit don't replace each other; they complete each other.

Jesus didn't say, "Born of Spirit only." He said, *"Born of water AND Spirit"* (John 3:5).

The Spirit is breath and fire. The water is appointed witness. You cannot dismiss what Jesus joined and call it maturity

9. The Sprinkler System Cow

When a Cup Tries to Replace a River. Another cow tiptoes through church history insisting that sprinkling, pouring, misting, spritzing, or holy water droplets flung from the fingertips of a well-meaning minister "count" as baptism.

Biblically, that claim has a hard time standing.

Now, to be fair, Scripture does contain sprinkling rites. Under Moses, some purifications were administered by sprinkling - especially in connection with the water of purification and covenant cleansing (Numbers 19:13, 18–21; Hebrews 9:13, 19, 21). Ezekiel also used sprinkling as prophetic language for cleansing:

"Then will I sprinkle clean water upon you, and ye shall be clean" (Ezekiel 36:25).

But Scripture does not treat every purification as the same kind of washing. Other acts of consecration and ceremonial cleansing required the body to be washed or bathed in water

(Exodus 29:4; Leviticus 14:8–9; Leviticus 15:5–13; Leviticus 16:4). Hebrews itself preserves that distinction when it speaks of hearts "sprinkled from an evil conscience" and bodies "washed with pure water" (Hebrews 10:22). That distinction matters. Scripture knows the difference between sprinkling and washing. And when the New Testament stops speaking in priestly imagery and starts showing baptism itself, it repeatedly reaches for the washing/immersion side of the picture - much water (John 3:23), going down into the water and coming up out of it (Acts 8:38–39), and burial with Christ (Romans 6:3–4; Colossians 2:12).

The Greek word *baptizō* does not mean "lightly moisturize." It means immerse. Submerge. [66] [67] [68] Drown the old man and raise the new one. (Matthew 3:16; Mark 1:10; Acts 8:38-39; John 3:23; Romans 6:3-4; Colossians 2:12)

Paul said baptism is burial (Romans 6:3–4). Try burying someone with a tablespoon of dirt and see how long it takes before they sit up again.

Sprinkling struggles to teach burial with the same force immersion naturally carries.

---

[66] Justin Martyr. (1885). *The First Apology*, ch. 61. In A. Roberts & J. Donaldson (Eds.), *Ante-Nicene Fathers* (Vol. 1). Buffalo, NY: Christian Literature Publishing Co. (Text via New Advent).
[67] *The Didache (Teaching of the Twelve Apostles)*. (c. 1st–2nd century). Ch. 7 (Baptism instructions). (Translation text).
[68] Thayer, J. H. (1889). *A Greek-English Lexicon of the New Testament*. New York, NY: American Book Company. Entry: βαπτίζω (baptizo)

John didn't stand on the bank with a ladle. Jesus didn't get a drizzle. Philip didn't pour bottled water over the Ethiopian. "Both went down into the water." (Acts 8:38)

The point is not aesthetics. The point is that Scripture keeps reaching for immersion when it speaks about baptismal witness.

10. The Thief-on-the-Cross Cow

When Paradise Is Mistaken for Heaven

This cow is often rolled out as the final argument against baptism:

"The thief on the cross wasn't baptized, and Jesus said, 'Today you will be with Me in paradise.' Therefore baptism isn't necessary." That conclusion only works if *paradise* means *heaven*.

Scripture says it does not.

Paradise Was Not Heaven - Not Yet

According to many Jewish conceptions in Jesus' day, Sheol was the realm of the dead, and it was not imagined as a single, undifferentiated experience. Scripture itself speaks of Sheol as a real domain (e.g., "*You will not abandon my soul to Sheol*" - Psalm 16:10), and it also pairs Sheol with Abaddon - "destruction" - to describe the depths of death's domain (Job 26:6; Proverbs 15:11). Jesus drew on this familiar framework when He described a place of comfort with Abraham (Abraham's bosom) distinct from a place of torment in the account of Lazarus and the rich man (Luke 16:19–31). In that conceptual world, "paradise" would be heard as the comfort-side of the dead, rest with the righteous, distinct from torment and from Abaddon's destructive depth, until the final resurrection and judgment. [69] [70] [71] [72] [73]

Lazarus did not go to heaven. He went to Abraham's bosom.

The rich man did not go to heaven. He went to torment.

Both were in Sheol - separated, conscious, and awaiting redemption.

This matters, because Jesus did not ascend to heaven that day either.

Scripture is explicit:

- Jesus descended into the lower parts of the earth (Ephesians 4:9)

- He preached to the spirits in prison (1 Peter 3:18–20)

---

[69]Kohler, K. (1906). *Abraham's bosom*. In I. Singer (Ed.), The Jewish encyclopedia. New York, NY: Funk & Wagnalls.

[70] Nickelsburg, G. W. E., & VanderKam, J. C. (2012). 1 Enoch: A new translation. Minneapolis, MN: Fortress Press. *(See especially the section commonly cited as 1 Enoch 22 for "separated places" for the dead.)*

[71] Stone, M. E. (1990). Fourth Ezra: A commentary on the book of Fourth Ezra. Minneapolis, MN: Fortress Press. *(Discusses afterlife "stores/chambers" imagery often cited from 4 Ezra 7.)*

[72] van der Toorn, K., Becking, B., & van der Horst, P. W. (Eds.). (1999). Dictionary of deities and demons in the Bible (2nd ed.). Grand Rapids, MI: Eerdmans; Leiden, Netherlands: Brill. *(Entry: "Abaddon.")*

[73] Wright, N. T. (2003). The resurrection of the Son of God. Minneapolis, MN: Fortress Press

- He did not ascend to the Father until after the resurrection (John 20:17)

If *paradise* meant heaven, then Jesus would have had to lie - because He Himself did not go there that day.

He didn't.

Where the Thief Actually Went

The thief went exactly where Jesus said He would go:

Paradise. Abraham's bosom. The place of waiting - not the place of enthronement.

The thief was not experiencing New Covenant salvation. He was receiving Old Covenant mercy at the threshold of fulfillment.

The blood had not yet been shed. The veil had not yet been torn. The covenant had not yet been inaugurated.

Hebrews is clear: *"A covenant is not in force while the one who made it is still alive."* (Hebrews 9:16–17)

The thief died before:

- the blood spoke remission

- baptism was commanded in Christ's Name

- the gospel was preached in its full form

- the Kingdom was opened to all nations

He was saved (sōzō - restored) *to the extent available at that moment* - not according to a pattern that had not yet been revealed.

Mercy Is Not a Template

Jesus had authority on earth to forgive sins directly (Mark 2:10). That authority does not eliminate later obedience - it establishes it.

The thief is an example of **Christ's compassion**, not **Christ's commission**.

If the thief's moment defines doctrine, then:

- baptism becomes optional

- resurrection becomes secondary

- and obedience becomes situational

Scripture never tells us to imitate the thief.

It tells us to obey the risen Christ.

Why This Cow Still Matters

The thief did not bypass baptism into heaven. He entered the place of waiting with Christ - until the blood finished its work.

After the resurrection, the message changed.

Now repentance is preached. Now baptism is commanded. Now remission is declared.

Not because mercy disappeared - but because covenant was completed.

Paradise was temporary. The Kingdom is permanent.

Bottom Line

The thief did not disprove baptism. He proved that until the blood was shed, even the righteous waited.

An exception explains mercy. Command establishes obedience.

And the risen Christ did not leave us with the thief's exception as our rule. He gave the Church a command.

11. The "Heaven Is the Goal" Cow

When Salvation Is Reduced to an Exit Plan

This cow quietly reshaped modern Christianity.

It teaches that salvation's primary purpose is getting people *out* of earth and *into* heaven.

But Scripture doesn't frame salvation as escape - it frames it as a future inheritance.

The word *sōzō* does not mean "admitted into heaven." It means to heal, rescue, make whole, restore.

Jesus didn't preach, "The Kingdom is where you're going." He preached, *"The Kingdom is at hand."* (Matthew 4:17)

Baptism doesn't prepare you to die. It prepares you to live differently.

Romans 6 doesn't say you were baptized to leave the world - it says you were baptized to walk in newness of life.

When heaven becomes the goal, obedience becomes optional. But when restoration is the goal, baptism becomes essential.

12. The Faith-without-Obedience Cow

When Belief Is Treated as Completion

This cow quotes verses about faith and ignores everything that follows them.

It says, "All that matters is believing."

Scripture says believing is where things begin, not where they end.

Jesus said, *"He that believes and is baptized…"* (Mark 16:16). James said faith without obedience is dead (James 2:17). Hebrews says Jesus is the author of salvation to those who obey Him (Hebrews 5:9).

Belief that never moves the body has not yet captured the heart.

Baptism is not an add-on to faith - it is faith taking physical form.

Obedience does not compete with grace. It is the human response to grace already expressed.

13. The "Baptism Replaces Discipleship" Cow

When the Womb Is Treated Like the Finish Line

This cow celebrates baptism and forgets everything that comes after.

"You're baptized? Great - you're done."

Scripture never treats baptism as graduation.

Baptism is birth. Birth is not maturity - it is responsibility.

Jesus was baptized *before* ministry. The apostles were baptized *before* mission. The early church was baptized *before* persecution, formation, and fruit.

Baptism does not end the journey - it starts it.

Water breaks. The Spirit breathes. Life begins.

If baptism is the finish line, fruit is optional. But Scripture says fruit is expected (Matthew 3:8; John 15:8).

14. The "Spirit Without Structure" Cow

When Fire Is Expected Without Preparation

This cow insists that spiritual power can be poured into unaligned vessels.

Scripture never supports that.

In the Old Testament:

- priests were washed **before** they were anointed
- altars were prepared **before** fire fell

In the New Testament:

- repentance precedes baptism

- baptism precedes empowerment
- obedience precedes authority

Fire does not fall on disorder. It falls on surrender.

The Spirit does not make surrender unnecessary. It honors what God has ordered.

15. The "Tradition Equals Truth" Cow

When Longevity Is Confused with Authority

This cow says, *"We've always done it this way."* But Scripture never measures truth by age. It measures truth by witness.

Jesus confronted traditions older than Rome and exposed what they had done to God's intent: *"You shut up the kingdom of heaven against men; for you neither enter yourselves, nor allow those who are entering to go in."* (Matthew 23:13)

The problem was not zeal. It was tradition elevated to authority.

Again He said, *"Why do you transgress the commandment of God because of your tradition?"* (Matthew 15:3) And later, *"Thus you have made the commandment of God of no effect by your tradition."* (Matthew 15:6)

That is the danger of this cow: tradition doesn't merely *add* - it can neutralize.

Paul addressed the same issue in a different generation: *"See to it that no one takes you captive through philosophy and empty deceit, according to the tradition of men… and not according to Christ.”* (Colossians 2:8)

Tradition is not evil. But Scripture never grants it equality with revelation.

Jesus did not condemn Moses. He condemned traditions that *claimed* to honor Moses while quietly contradicting God's intent.

Paul likewise warned that customs, practices, and teachings - even sincere ones - must remain accountable to what was first delivered: *"If anyone thinks himself to be spiritual, let him acknowledge that the things I write are the commandments of the Lord."* (1 Corinthians 14:37)

Tradition may preserve memory. Only truth preserves life.

When tradition aligns with Scripture, it serves. When tradition contradicts witness, tradition yields.

This cow is not on the grill because it is old. It is on the grill because it refuses correction.

15. The "The Word Replaced the Water" Cow
When Scripture Is Used to Fire the River

This cow sounds spiritual. It quotes Paul. It carries a Bible. And it quietly removes baptism while insisting it's honoring Scripture.

The argument goes like this: "Paul said Christ cleanses the Church by the *washing of water by the Word (rhema)* (Ephesians 5:26).

Therefore, the Word (*rhema*) replaces water. Baptism is unnecessary once Scripture is received."

That sounds tidy. It is also grammatically careless and biblically unsound.

Paul did not say the Word (*rhema or logos*) replaces water. He said the washing is water - and that it occurs in connection with the Word (*rhema*).

The Greek phrase is:

τῷ λουτρῷ τοῦ ὕδατος ἐν ῥήματι "the washing of water in / in response to / in connection with the spoken word (*rhema*)"

Paul does not use *logos* here (written Word). He uses *rhema* - revealed, spoken Word that awakens faith (Romans 10:17).

The Word (*rhema or logos*) does not do the washing. The Word (*rhema*) awakens the heart that obeys the washing.

If Scripture replaced baptism:

- Jesus would not have commanded it (Matthew 28:19)
- Peter would not have preached it (Acts 2:38)
- Paul would not have practiced it (Acts 19:1–6)
- The Spirit would not have required it after falling (Acts 10:47–48)

Paul never fired the river. He explained why the river works.

The Word (*logos*) conceives

The Word (*rhema*) awakens

The water delivers.

269

The Spirit indwells.

The Blood authorizes.

Remove the water, and you don't get deeper revelation - you get disembodied faith.

This cow confuses awakening with obedience. It treats cognition as covenant and replaces surrender with study.

But Scripture never teaches that reading replaces responding. Revelation does not cancel obedience - it calls for it.

If *"washing of water by the Word"* meant baptism was obsolete, then Paul contradicted:

- Jesus (Matthew 28:19)
- Peter (Acts 2:38)
- Himself (Romans 6:3–4; Colossians 2:11–12)

Paul was not spiritualizing baptism away. He was locating it correctly - as the outward witness to an inward awakening.

The Word (*logos* or *rhema*) does not replace the water. The Word (*rhema*) leads you to it.

This cow can leave the pasture now.

16. The "First Works = Get Re-Baptized" Cow (33)

When Revelation 2:5 Is Turned into a Dunk-Again Doctrine

This cow shows up wearing a prophetic cape and saying, "You've left your first love, so go do your first works… which means: get baptized again."

It sounds urgent. It sounds spiritual. It even quotes Scripture.

But it's built on an assumption Revelation never states.

What Jesus Actually Said

Jesus told the church at Ephesus:

"Remember therefore from whence thou art fallen, and repent, and do the first works…" (Revelation 2:5)

Notice what He did **not** say:

- He didn't say, "Return to your first ordinance."
- He didn't say, "Repeat your baptism."
- He didn't say, "Go back to the water."

He said:

- remember
- repent
- return to your first works

That is relational language, not ritual language. Ephesus didn't lose a ceremony, they lost their love. The correction is not "redo your initiation," but "restore your devotion."

And the *reason* He says it is explicit: *"You have left your first love."* (Revelation 2:4)

That is not a water-problem. That is a love-problem. A drift-problem. A devotion-problem.

If "first works" meant "get baptized again," the remedy would read like Acts, clear, direct, un-mystical: *repent… be baptized…* (Acts 2:38). But Revelation 2:5 doesn't talk like Acts, because it isn't addressing the same moment.

What are "first works" in the context? The works that flowed from first love, the early obedience, the early tenderness, the early alignment that once made their labor clean instead of mechanical (compare Revelation 2:2–4). In other words: return to the relational posture that birthed the obedience, not to a ritual as if ritual could manufacture love.

Yes, people sometimes return to water because revelation deepens, conscience awakens, or alignment clarifies (Acts 19:1–6). That's a separate discussion, and it is handled carefully elsewhere in this book.

But using Revelation 2:5 as a "rebaptism command" asks the verse to carry more than it was given to carry. [74]

The First Works Were Love-Works

In the New Testament, "works" are repeatedly framed as the fruit that flows from repentance and love, acts of obedience, faith, endurance, service, generosity, and faithfulness. Ephesus was commended for labor and endurance (Revelation 2:2–3), but corrected for leaving love (Revelation 2:4). The remedy is not a new dip, it is a return to love that produces works.

---

[74] This "first works = rebaptism" reading is not new. It shows up in documented mid-20th-century American religious print as an established interpretive move, presented as a corrective return to "first works."

Baptism is a commanded act of obedience, yes. But baptism is not the universal translation key for every verse that contains the word "works."

Why This Misreading Spreads

This cow survives because it uses a familiar move:

1. Find a verse that says "repent" and "works."
2. Assume "works" must mean "baptism."
3. Turn a relational correction into an ordinance requirement.

But Revelation 2:5 is not a baptism text. It is a repentance-and-return text.

A Simple Test

If "first works" *must* mean "baptism," then Jesus would be telling Ephesus:

- "Repent… and get baptized again… or I'll remove your lampstand."

That would make baptism the single required response to relational drift. Scripture never teaches that. When believers drift, Scripture calls them to repentance, renewal, obedience, and return, not automatically to re-immersion.

Repetition may be appropriate when revelation deepens (see Cow #3). But you don't build a rebaptism doctrine on a verse that never mentions water.

Bottom Line

Revelation 2:5 does not command rebaptism. It commands return, to love, to obedience, to the works that love produces.

But "new" doesn't mean "true." [75] Context does. The scriptural misconception surrounding this verse first appeared in 1943 in the Mormon Church (33).

This cow is grilled.

Final Word

If you recognize one of your old beliefs here, don't panic.

God is not offended by growth. He is pleased by humility.

This appendix is not a rebuke - it is an invitation. An invitation to see more clearly. To walk more fully. To align more deeply.

And if Aquila and Priscilla ever pull you aside and say, "Let us explain the way more perfectly," receive it the way Apollos did.

Not with shame. With hunger.

---

[75] And like all well-fed sacred cows, this one periodically wanders back into the pasture wearing "NEW REVELATION" on its forehead, despite being an old argument with fresh paint.

Appendix F

What This Book Is Not Saying

Before we go any further, a moment of clarity.

This book makes strong claims - not because it loves controversy, but because Scripture does. When long-held traditions are examined under the light of witness, some assumptions wobble. That can feel uncomfortable, especially if these ideas touch things we've been taught, cherished, or built our faith upon.

So let's be clear about what this book is not doing.

This section exists to create understanding, not division - to name the lines this book does *not* cross, even while it challenges some we've drawn ourselves.

This Book Is *Not* Teaching Baptismal Regeneration

This book does not teach that water itself saves, regenerates, or imparts life by chemistry, ritual, or sacrament.

Water does not forgive sins. Water does not create faith. Water does not replace the cross.

Scripture is clear: *life is in the blood* (Leviticus 17:11), and remission comes only through the blood of Christ (Hebrews 9:22). Baptism does not generate eternal salvation, a ticket to heaven, or restoration; it bears witness to what God has already initiated through repentance, faith, and covenantal obedience.

If baptism were regenerative by itself, then faith, repentance, the Word (*logos*), the revealed Word (*rhema*), and the testimony of the blood would be unnecessary. Scripture never allows that.

This book does not teach mechanisms. It teaches witness, alignment, and response.

Baptism is not the cause of life – it is the earthly testimony that a life has come under the reign of the King.

This Book Is *Not* Teaching Salvation by Works

Obedience is not payment. Submission is not currency. Getting wet is not earning grace.

This book does not teach that baptism is a work that purchases salvation. It teaches that baptism is a response to revelation, not a transaction for favor.

Grace initiates. Faith responds. Obedience aligns.

Works attempt to move God. Obedience responds to where God is already moving.

Baptism is not the cause of salvation - it is the agreement of the body with what heaven has already spoken.

This Book Is *Not* Denying the Role of Faith

Faith is essential. Faith precedes obedience. Faith without revelation does not exist.

This book does not minimize faith - it locates it properly. Faith is not mental assent alone; it is trust that moves the whole person toward alignment with God's will.

Scripture never separates faith from response. Faith hears. Faith turns. Faith obeys.

Baptism without faith is a bath. Faith without obedience is unfinished.

This book insists on keeping them together.

This Book Is *Not* Anti-Grace

Grace is not weakened here - it is clarified.

Grace is not a substance that "does the work." Grace is God's favorable disposition toward humanity - His initiative, His invitation, His mercy moving toward us.

Grace does not act; God acts in grace.

It is grace that moves God to draw near to man.

It is grace that moves God to reveal Himself in Word (*logos* and *rhema*) and deed.

It is grace that moves God to invite us into His family.

Obedience does not compete with grace. It is the human response to grace already expressed.

If grace never leads to obedience, it has not been received - it has only been recognized without yielding.

This Book Is *Not* Denying the Holy Spirit

This book does not deny the Spirit's work. It refuses only to detach the Spirit from Scripture's witness pattern.

The Spirit draws, convicts, breathes, empowers, and confirms - always in harmony with the Word (*logos*) and the blood. The Spirit is not a replacement for water, nor is water a substitute for the Spirit.

They work together.

Born of water and Spirit (John 3:5) was not a suggestion. It was a design.

This Book Is *Not* Declaring Past Believers "Unsaved"

This is crucial.

This book does not declare that those who followed Christ sincerely - even imperfectly - were false believers, lost, or deceived.

God honors faith where it is found. God meets people in the light they have.

But Scripture also records moments when greater clarity arrived - and faithful people adjusted their response accordingly (Acts 18:24–26; Acts 19:1–6).

Correction is not condemnation. Growth is not betrayal. Seeing more clearly does not invalidate earlier steps - it completes them.

Why This Clarification Matters

This book is not a weapon. It is not a gatekeeper. It is not a purity test.

It is an invitation to examine baptism the way Scripture presents it - not as a tradition to defend, but as a witness to honor.

The goal is harmony with heaven, not victory over one another.

If at any point this book unsettles you, that does not mean it is attacking your faith. It may simply be doing what Scripture has always done best:

Calling sincere people to see more perfectly.

Appendix G

Household Baptism: Covenant, Authority, and What Luke Was Actually Saying

Few passages generate more confusion than the household baptisms recorded in Acts. They are often invoked as proof-texts - either to defend infant baptism or to dismiss baptism's covenantal weight altogether.

Neither move does justice to the text.

To understand household baptism, we must stop reading Acts through modern individualism and return to the ancient worldview Luke assumed his readers already understood.

The World Luke Was Writing Into

In the Roman world, a household (*oikos*) was not merely a collection of individuals living under one roof. It was a legal, economic, and covenantal unit.

A household included:

- The head of the house
- His spouse
- Children
- Servants
- Dependents

- Sometimes extended family

The head of the household bore legal responsibility for everyone under his authority. If something happened on his watch, he answered for it - sometimes with his life.

This context is not an optional background. It is essential to understanding Acts.

Why the Jailer Was Panicking

When the Philippian jailer cried out,

"What must I do to be saved?" (Acts 16:30) He was not asking an abstract theological question.

Under Roman law, a jailer who lost prisoners faced execution, often along with severe consequences for his household. (18–20) When the prison doors opened, his life - and potentially his family's - was already forfeit.

This is why he was preparing to kill himself.

Paul's response reached deeper than the immediate crisis. Yes, the prisoners were still there - but Paul addressed a greater rescue than physical survival. The jailer had just been spared death, but he was being invited into covenant life.

Luke tells us that very night:

"He was baptized, he and all his household." (Acts 16:33)

This was not accidental. It was covenantal.

Why Luke Repeats Household Baptisms

Luke records multiple household baptisms:

- Lydia and her household (Acts 16:15)

- The Philippian jailer and his household (Acts 16:33)

- Cornelius' household (Acts 10:44–48)

- Crispus' household (Acts 18:8)

This repetition is intentional.

Luke is showing how Kingdom authority moves through covenant heads - not as coercion, but as corporate alignment. When revelation enters a house, it does not stop at the threshold.

What Household Baptism *Does Not* Automatically Mean

Household baptism does not require us to assume:

- That infants were baptized

- That repentance was bypassed

- That faith was unnecessary

- That baptism functioned magically

Luke never says infants were baptized. He never says repentance was skipped. He never says faith was absent.

In fact, Luke repeatedly emphasizes that the Word (*logos*) was spoken to the household, and that belief followed (Acts 16:32; Acts 18:8).

Household baptism is not a loophole around repentance - it is a demonstration of covenantal authority responding to revelation.

What Household Baptism *Does* Mean

Household baptism does show us something modern readers often miss:

1. Covenant operates corporately, not just individually

2. Authority carries responsibility downward

3. Obedience often moves faster than modern theological caution

In Scripture, when a household head aligned with God's covenant, the house moved with him - just as it did under Abraham, Joshua, and David.

"As for me and my house, we will serve the Lord." (Joshua 24:15)

That statement was not symbolic. It was authoritative.

Why This Does Not Undermine Personal Faith

Household baptism does not eliminate personal faith any more than circumcision eliminated personal obedience under the Old Covenant.

Covenant brings people into alignment. Faith matures within that alignment.

Children grow into faith. Servants respond to truth. Households learn together.

Luke is not denying individual response - he is showing how God often starts with authority to reach individuals.

Why Luke Includes This for Gentile Readers

Luke was writing primarily to Gentiles - people who already understood household authority.

To them, these stories made perfect sense.

They do not bypass the Word being spoken to the household, belief being present, or covenantal structure replacing personal faith

What confuses modern readers is not Luke's writing - it is our assumption that covenant must be individualistic to be authentic.

Scripture never makes that demand.

The Real Point Luke Is Making

Household baptism is not about age. It is not about infants. It is not about shortcuts.

It is about how revelation moves through authority.

When the head of a household encounters Christ, the river does not stop with him. It flows outward - into relationships, responsibility, and shared obedience.

That is not coercion.

That is covenant.

Why This Matters for Today

Household baptism reminds us that:

- Faith is personal, but obedience is often communal

- God honors authority structures without erasing individual conscience
- Baptism was never designed to be isolated from real life

The early church did not wait for perfect theological symmetry. When heaven moved, households moved with it.

And the water bore witness.

Appendix H

Sōzō and Sōtēria: Rescue, Formation, and Inheritance

Why This Appendix Exists

One of the greatest points of confusion in modern Christianity is not baptism, faith, or obedience - it is language. In particular, the English word *salvation* has been asked to carry meanings Scripture never assigned to it.

This appendix exists to restore biblical precision, not to dismantle anyone's faith.

Scripture speaks carefully. We must do the same.

Two Greek Words - One English Problem

The New Testament regularly uses two related but distinct Greek terms that English translations often flatten into one word.

sōzō (σῴζω) - verb

To rescue, heal, restore, deliver, preserve, make whole.

sōtēria (σωτηρία) - noun

Salvation/deliverance as an *outcome or state* -what "rescue" looks like when spoken of as something that arrives, is entered, is being received over time, and is ultimately unveiled.

These words are related - but they are not interchangeable. Scripture does not confuse them. Theology should not either.

sōzō - Rescue When the Kingdom Arrives

The verb **sōzō** describes what happens when God intervenes in real time.

It is:

- immediate

- situational

- restorative

- often visible in its effects

People are *saved* (sōzō) from:

- danger (Matthew 8:25)

- sickness (Mark 5:34)

- bondage (Luke 8:36)

- loss and ruin (Luke 19:9 – see note below)

sōzō is not a courtroom verdict. It is a rescue event.

It describes what happens when the Kingdom of God becomes present and active in a life. This is why Scripture can speak of people being "saved" in ways that are clearly present-tense and earthly: healed, restored, delivered, preserved:

- before the cross

- before Pentecost

- before any developed afterlife theology

They were rescued, not relocated.

Luke 19:9 - "Today Salvation Has Come to This House"

"Today salvation has come to this house, because he also is a son of Abraham."

This passage often raises concern, but the context resolves the tension.

What happened that day?

- Zacchaeus repented

- He restored what he had stolen

- He realigned his life under God's rule

- Jesus publicly affirmed that the Kingdom had entered his house

Luke uses the noun (sōtēria) - but the moment described is a Kingdom-arrival rescue in real time: a life brought back under God's reign. This was not a declaration of final inheritance. It was a present rescue and restoration.

In Luke's Gospel, *salvation coming* consistently means:

- deliverance has arrived

- authority has shifted

- a life has come back under God's reign

Zacchaeus experienced **sōzō** - rescue - not the end-of-the-age consummation.

sōtēria - Salvation Spoken in Three Movements

The New Testament speaks of sōtēria in more than one time-frame. That is not contradiction - it is how Scripture holds Kingdom reality and inheritance reality together.

1) Salvation as Present Arrival (entered now)

Sometimes salvation is spoken of as something that has come, is present, or is available now - the Kingdom arriving with rescue, restoration, and realignment.

Examples:

- "Now is the day of salvation (sōtēria)" (2 Corinthians 6:2)
- "Today salvation (sōtēria) has come to this house" (Luke 19:9)
- "My eyes have seen Your salvation (sōtērion)" (Luke 2:30)

This is salvation in the sense of God's reign breaking into a life.

2) Salvation as Ongoing Reception (already underway)

Sometimes salvation is spoken of as something being received in motion - real, present, working toward its intended end.

Example:

- "Receiving the end of your faith, the salvation (sōtēria) of your souls" (1 Peter 1:9)

This is crucial: Scripture can speak of salvation as being received, while still pointing toward "the end." Receiving does not always mean "finished." It can mean "actively being brought into."

3) Salvation as Future Unveiling (not yet fully manifested)

Sometimes salvation is framed as something nearer, ready to be revealed, or tied to Christ's appearing - language that places fullness on the horizon.

Examples:

- "Our salvation (sōtēria) is nearer now than when we first believed" (Romans 13:11)
- "A salvation (sōtēria) ready to be revealed in the last time" (1 Peter 1:5)
- "He will appear… for salvation (eis sōtērian) to those who eagerly wait for Him" (Hebrews 9:28)

This is salvation spoken of as inheritance unveiled - not merely rescue experienced.

Progressive Reality, Earnest, and Inheritance

Scripture repeatedly treats the Kingdom as something that arrives now and is lived under, while inheritance is something that is proved, formed, and finally unveiled.

The New Testament even speaks of the Spirit as an earnest / guarantee (a down payment) of what is coming (Ephesians 1:13–14; 2 Corinthians 1:22). That means the life of the Kingdom is not a static "ticket" - it is the beginning of an inheritance that must be faithfully carried.

This is why Scripture can hold these truths together without contradiction:

- rescue can be real now

- formation can be required over time

- inheritance can be unveiled later

Jesus' own teachings confirm this pattern:

- servants are judged **after** being entrusted

- branches are cut off **after** being connected

- sons can be disinherited **after** being in the house

To be *cast out*, one must first have entered. This is not instability. It is sonship.

Why Scripture Holds the Tension

The Bible intentionally holds these truths together:

- You can be rescued now and still warned later

- You can be saved today and judged tomorrow

- You can belong and still squander inheritance

Salvation is not a ticket. It is a life lived under authority.

How This Relates to Baptism

This book does not present baptism as:

- a ritual guaranteeing eternal destiny

- a substitute for faith

- a mechanical transaction

Instead, baptism consistently appears in Scripture as a response to rescue already initiated.

- Acts 2:38 - repentance and baptism follow awakening

- Acts 22:16 - obedience follows revelation

- Acts 8, Acts 10, Acts 16, Acts 19 - water answers what God has already begun

Baptism:

- does **not** cause rescue (sōzō)

- does **not** complete inheritance (sōtēria)

- bears witness to a life turning under Kingdom authority

- positions a person on the path where inheritance is formed and proved.

Salvation Is Not the Gospel - the Kingdom Is

Jesus did not preach *salvation* as the message.

He preached:

- "The Kingdom of God is at hand"

- "Repent"

- "Follow Me"

Rescue (sōzō) is what happens when the Kingdom arrives.

Salvation as outcome (sōtēria) is what Scripture often speaks of as unfolding and finally unveiled as the Kingdom is faithfully lived under.

This is why Scripture speaks of:

- saved people who later fall away
- servants cast out
- branches removed
- sheep and goats separated

Judgment assumes participation. Inheritance assumes faithfulness.

What This Book Is - and Is Not - Saying

This book does not deny:

- faith
- grace
- the cross
- eternal inheritance
- future judgment

It does insist that:

- Scripture treats rescue (sōzō) as present and lived
- Scripture often frames salvation-as-outcome (sōtēria) as future-facing, weighty, and perseverance
- baptism belongs to sonship formation, not ritual assurance

If this distinction feels uncomfortable, it is likely because modern theology trained us to expect finality where Scripture taught formation.

For Further Study

This appendix intentionally remains concise.

A full biblical, linguistic, and theological exploration of:

- sōzō
- sōtēria
- judgment
- inheritance
- Kingdom formation

is developed in the companion volume:

Sōzō: What Am I Saved From?

These two books are designed to work together, not compete.

Appendix H References

Bauer, W., Danker, F. W., Arndt, W. F., & Gingrich, F. W. (2000). *A Greek-English lexicon of the New Testament and other early Christian literature* (3rd ed.). University of Chicago Press.

Eynikel, E., Lust, J., & Hauspie, K. (2003). *A Greek-English lexicon of the Septuagint* (Rev. ed.). Deutsche Bibelgesellschaft.

Kittel, G., & Friedrich, G. (Eds.). (1964–1976). *Theological dictionary of the New Testament* (G. W. Bromiley, Trans.; Vols. 1–10). Wm. B. Eerdmans.

Liddell, H. G., Scott, R., Jones, H. S., & McKenzie, R. (1996). *A Greek-English lexicon* (9th ed. with revised supplement). Clarendon Press.

Louw, J. P., & Nida, E. A. (1989). *Greek-English lexicon of the New Testament: Based on semantic domains* (2nd ed., Vols. 1–2). United Bible Societies.

Moulton, J. H., & Milligan, G. (1930). *The vocabulary of the Greek Testament: Illustrated from the papyri and other non-literary sources.* Hodder & Stoughton.

Mounce, W. D. (2006). *Mounce's complete expository dictionary of Old and New Testament words.* Zondervan.

Appendix I

Repeated Washings and the Rise of Rebaptism Prohibition

Why This Appendix Exists

I did not include this appendix because rebaptism is the center of this book. It is not. I included it because, while writing, I kept running into a level of resistance that far exceeded ordinary disagreement. I have seen the subject stir suspicion, split churches, wound ministers, and push people out of fellowship, which forced me to ask an honest question: why does the mere mention of a later baptism provoke so much heat? This appendix exists to answer that question as fairly as possible, by tracing the biblical and historical record and showing that the controversy over rebaptism has often been about far more than water alone.

Introduction

People speak of rebaptism as though Scripture settled the matter with one cold sentence and shut the door forever. Scripture is not that thin. The world out of which baptism comes was already full of water with purpose. Priests washed. The unclean washed. Israel knew repeated ordinances of cleansing, readiness, and return. Hebrews does not describe that older order as a single act, but as a system marked by "various washings." [76]

The New Testament does not flatten that world. It gathers it into Christ. John's baptism was not identical in purpose to baptism in Jesus' name. Hebrews still speaks in the plural language of "baptisms" or washings. Acts 19 shows men who had received John's baptism later entering the water again under fuller revelation in Christ. That does not make every later immersion right. It does make one thing plain: Scripture itself does not treat every later baptism as an obvious sin. [77]

Church history shows the same complexity. In the third century, Cyprian argued that baptism outside the true church was not baptism at all. That means one of the earliest major fights was not over whether every second washing was sinful, but over who had the authority to call the first one valid. The dispute with Stephen of Rome sharpened the point even further. Stephen insisted that nothing be "innovated" and recognized heretical baptism as valid; Cyprian and his allies refused. Later historical summaries report that Stephen broke communion with Cyprian and Carthage over the issue. The argument had already become a struggle over jurisdiction and authority, not simply over water. [78]

---

[76] Exodus 30:18–21; Leviticus. 14:8–9; Numbers. 19:7, 19; Hebrews. 9:10.
[77] Hebrews 6:2; Matthew 3:11; Acts 19:1–6.
[78] Cyprian, *Epistle 72* and *Epistle 73*. Cyprian explicitly argued that baptism outside the Church was not "valid or legitimate," while Stephen of Rome insisted that nothing be "innovated." Later historical summaries state that Stephen broke communion with Cyprian and Carthage over the controversy.

The anti-Donatist struggle hardened that instinct. Augustine argued that baptism belongs to Christ rather than to the worthiness of the minister, and the Council of Arles again condemned the Donatists. What followed was not merely a theological disagreement. Britannica records that after the 411 conference at Carthage, severe laws denied the Donatists both civil and ecclesiastical rights. By then, the issue had moved far beyond the question of what happened in the water. It had become a machinery for deciding who belonged, who did not, and who had the right to say so. [79]

Later sacramental systems turned that control into law. Roman Catholic teaching says baptism leaves an indelible character, is given once for all, and cannot be repeated; canon law says baptism, confirmation, and orders cannot be repeated, except conditionally when validity is in prudent doubt. Trent went further and attached anathema to repeating a baptism deemed true and rightly administered, and even to requiring later ratification of infant baptism; in one canon it also envisions exclusion from the Eucharist and other sacraments as a penalty. At that point, a later baptism was no longer heard merely as a fresh act of obedience. It was heard as a direct challenge to the Church's sacramental claims and disciplinary authority. [80]

---

[79] Augustine, *On Baptism, Against the Donatists*; *Council of Arles* (314). On the legal consequences after the Donatist controversy, see *Encyclopaedia Britannica*, "Donatists."
[80] *Catechism of the Catholic Church*, §§1272–1274; *Code of Canon Law*, can. 845 §1; *Council of Trent*, Session VII, Canons 9, 11, 13, and 14.

And this was not a polite quarrel in a council chamber. It was bloody. In the first generation of the Anabaptist movement, Britannica notes that what authorities regarded as a second baptism was a crime punishable by death. Zürich made adult rebaptism a capital offense in 1526, and Felix Manz was executed by drowning in 1527. The language of rebaptism was not only theological; it was judicial, political, and lethal. It marked people for punishment. To tell this story as though it were only a civilized disagreement between interpreters is to wash the blood off the stones too quickly. [81]

Modern evangelical objections usually do not take such violent form, but the instinct can still be similar. In many churches, baptism is described as symbolic and non-saving, yet still treated as the one public witness of a once-for-all conversion. The *Baptist Faith and Message* defines baptism as an act of obedience symbolizing faith while also teaching that true believers endure to the end. Grace Community Church teaches that the redeemed are secure in Christ forever. Ligonier warns that baptizing more than once may suggest regeneration is repeatable, and Desiring God counsels believers to find grace not in being re-baptized but in remembering their one baptism. In that setting, resistance to a

---

[81] *Encyclopaedia Britannica*, "Anabaptist"; World History Encyclopedia, "Zwingli's Persecution of the Anabaptists." Britannica notes that what authorities regarded as a second baptism was punishable by death; the Zürich mandate of March 7, 1526, made adult rebaptism a capital offense by drowning.

later baptism often functions as a defense of assurance, permanence, and the finality attached to the first saving response.[82]

Even later examples make the same point. The Church of Jesus Christ of Latter-day Saints acknowledges that nineteenth-century Latter-day Saints practiced rebaptism for renewal of covenants, healing, and restoration to fellowship, and says that most Saints in nineteenth-century Utah were rebaptized several times throughout their lives. That example does not create the issue, and it should not be used as a cheap dismissal of every Christian conversation about later baptism. It simply shows that repeated water has continued to reappear wherever people believed one immersion could not exhaust every covenantal purpose attached to obedience, renewal, and belonging. [83]

So the better question is not, "Has this body been in water before?" The better question is, "What was that washing, what did it mean, who declared it valid, and what is God requiring now?" Once that question is asked honestly, the blanket prohibition begins to look less like a plain command of Scripture and more like a fence built by tradition around a subject the Bible itself leaves more textured, layered, and alive. History does not prove that every repeated immersion is wise. But it does prove that the harshest rhetoric against rebaptism has repeatedly been tied to

----

[82] *Baptist Faith and Message* 2000, arts. V and VII; Grace Community Church, "Doctrinal Statement"; Ligonier Ministries, "One Baptism"; Mathis, "Improving Our Baptism."
[83] The Church of Jesus Christ of Latter-day Saints, "Rebaptism."

institutional power: breaking communion, condemning rivals, denying rights, excluding from sacraments, and in some eras spilling blood. [84]

References

Augustine. (n.d.). *On baptism, against the Donatists.* New Advent. https://www.newadvent.org/fathers/1408.htm

Cyprian of Carthage. (n.d.). *Epistle 72: To Jubaianus, concerning the baptism of heretics.* New Advent. https://www.newadvent.org/fathers/050672.htm

Cyprian of Carthage. (n.d.). *Epistle 73: To Pompey, against the epistle of Stephen about the baptism of heretics.* New Advent. https://www.newadvent.org/fathers/050673.htm

Encyclopaedia Britannica. (n.d.). *Anabaptist.* https://www.britannica.com/topic/Anabaptists

Encyclopaedia Britannica. (n.d.). *Council of Arles.* https://www.britannica.com/event/Council-of-Arles

Encyclopaedia Britannica. (n.d.). *Donatists.* https://www.britannica.com/topic/Donatists

Grace Community Church. (2024, May 6). *Doctrinal statement.* https://www.gracechurch.org/about/doctrinal-statement

---

[84] This conclusion is a historical inference drawn from the sources above. The record shows that the controversy over rebaptism repeatedly involved questions of validity, communion, discipline, sacramental authority, civil standing, and coercive power, not merely the meaning of water.

Ligonier Ministries. (2017, October 16). *One baptism.*
https://learn.ligonier.org/devotionals/one-baptism

Mathis, D. (2012, November 15). *Improving our baptism.* Desiring
God. https://www.desiringgod.org/articles/improving-
our-baptism

Southern Baptist Convention. (2023). *Baptist Faith and Message
2000.* https://bfm.sbc.net/bfm2000/

The Church of Jesus Christ of Latter-day Saints. (n.d.). *Rebaptism.*
https://www.churchofjesuschrist.org/study/history/topics
/rebaptism?lang=eng

The Holy See. (1983). *Code of Canon Law*, canon 845.
https://press.vatican.va/archive/cod-iuris-
canonici/eng/documents/cic_lib4-cann834-878_en.html

The Holy See. (n.d.). *Catechism of the Catholic Church: The grace of
baptism.*
https://www.vatican.va/content/catechism/en/part_two/
section_two/chapter_one/article_1/vii_the_grace_of_bapt
ism.html

World History Encyclopedia. (2021, December 17). *Zwingli's
persecution of the Anabaptists.*
https://www.worldhistory.org/article/1932/zwinglis-
persecution-of-the-anabaptists/

Glossary of Terms

Baptism

Definition: Full immersion in water in obedience to Christ, an embodied act of surrender that aligns with His death, burial, and resurrection and stands under His authority and covenant.

Scripture: Matthew 28:19; Acts 2:38; Romans 6:3–4; Galatians 3:27

Clarification: Baptism is not a ritual securing an eternal destination. It is the **witnessed entry into covenant,** the embodied response to divine calling, and the moment a believer is identified as belonging to Christ under His authority.

Blood (Witness of the Blood)

Definition: The covenantal means by which God establishes redemption, removes guilt, and grants legal standing before Him.

Scripture: Hebrews 9:22; Hebrews 12:24; 1 John 5:6–8; Ephesians 1:7

Clarification: The blood does not act independently or autonomously; it functions according to God's decree. Scripture assigns the blood covenantal authority - not agency of its own. The blood establishes what water witnesses and what the Spirit confirms.

Covenant

Definition: A binding relational agreement initiated by God that establishes identity, inheritance, and obligation.

Scripture: Genesis 17:10–11; Jeremiah 31:31–34; Hebrews 8:6–13

Clarification: Covenant always involves cost, witness, and obedience. Baptism does not create covenant; it **acknowledges and enters into one already established by Christ**.

Grace (Charis)

Definition: God's favorable disposition toward humanity, expressed freely and unearned.

Scripture: Ephesians 2:8–9; Titus 2:11

Clarification: Grace is not a force that performs work. It is God's disposition that **moves the heart of the giver and invites response from the receiver**. Obedience does not compete with grace; it is the human response to grace already expressed.

Kingdom of God

Definition: The active reign and authority of God manifested on earth through obedient sons and daughters.

Scripture: Matthew 6:33; Luke 17:21; Romans 14:17

Clarification: The gospel proclaimed by Jesus was not about escape from earth but **Heaven's government arriving upon it**. Baptism marks alignment with this reign.

Logos (Word – Eternal)

Definition: The eternal, preexistent Word of God by whom all things were created and sustained.

Scripture: John 1:1–3; Colossians 1:16–17

Clarification: The Logos conceives life. It is the eternal record from which all divine action proceeds.

Rhema (Word – Revealed)

Definition: The spoken or revealed Word of God that awakens faith, conviction, and response.

Scripture: Romans 10:17; Jeremiah 23:29

Clarification: Rhema does not replace Logos; it **reveals Logos to the heart**. The revealed Word awakens repentance and draws the believer toward obedience, including baptism.

Repentance (Metanoia)

Definition: A Spirit-led change of mind that results in a decisive turning away from sin and a reorientation of life toward God's will.

Scripture: Acts 2:38; 2 Corinthians 7:10; Matthew 3:8

Clarification: Repentance is not regret. It is alignment. Baptism bears witness to repentance already begun.

Sonship

Definition: The restored identity of a believer as a legitimate child of God, brought into relationship, inheritance, and authority.

Scripture: Romans 8:15–17; Galatians 4:5–7; John 1:12

Clarification: Sonship is the goal of redemption. Baptism does not create sons; it **identifies and aligns those who have been called into sonship**.

Spirit (Pneuma – Breath)

Definition: The breath or wind of God proceeding from Him, imparting life, movement, and empowerment.

Scripture: Genesis 2:7; John 20:22; Acts 2:2–4

Clarification: Pneuma describes force and movement rather than autonomous personality. The Spirit acts when God breathes, moves where God directs, and is recognized by its effects - life, power, and transformation.

Witness

Definition: A confirming testimony established by agreement.

Scripture: Deuteronomy 19:15; 1 John 5:6–8

Clarification: In baptism, Scripture identifies three earthly witnesses: **the water, the Spirit, and the blood**. None initiate covenant; all testify to what God has already established.

Water (Witness of Water)

Definition: The physical element God repeatedly uses as a boundary marker of transition, cleansing, and new beginning.

Scripture: Genesis 1:2; Exodus 14; Matthew 3:13–17; Acts 8:38

Clarification: Water does not cleanse by power of its own. It bears witness to obedience, repentance, and covenantal transition.

Washing of Water by the Word

Definition: The process by which God cleanses and prepares His people through revealed truth and obedient response.

Scripture: Ephesians 5:26

Clarification: The Word (rhema) does not replace baptism; it summons obedience toward it. Revelation awakens and prepares the heart; the blood cleanses the conscience; the water bears witness to the response.

Shame

Definition: A false verdict of unworthiness rooted in sin, fear, or accusation.

Scripture: Romans 10:11; Hebrews 12:2

Clarification: Shame is broken when the conscience is cleansed by Christ's blood, and you step into the water in obedient agreement with that verdict; the Spirit bears witness to the new beginning.

Sōtēria (σωτηρία)

Definition: A Greek noun referring to salvation as inheritance, outcome, or completed deliverance.

Scripture: Romans 13:11; 1 Peter 1:9; Philippians 2:12; Hebrews 9:28

Clarification: In this book, *sōtēria* refers to **future-oriented inheritance** that unfolds through faithfulness, formation, and perseverance under the Kingdom of God. It is not a momentary event, but the culmination of a life lived in obedient sonship.

Sōzō (σῴζω)

Definition: A Greek verb meaning to rescue, heal, restore, deliver, or make whole.

Scripture: Luke 8:48; Luke 17:19; Matthew 8:25; James 5:15

Clarification: In this book, *sōzō* describes **present rescue and restoration** that occurs when the Kingdom of God becomes active in a person's life. It is not a statement about eternal destination, but an indicator of **Kingdom presence, authority shift, and lived transformation** under God's reign.

Submission

Definition: Yielding oneself to God's authority and order.

Scripture: James 4:7; Romans 6:16

Clarification: Authority flows from submission. Baptism is an act of embodied submission.

Witness of the Spirit

Definition: The confirming presence of God's breath that empowers and indwells believers.

Scripture: Romans 8:16; Acts 10:44–48

Clarification: The Spirit does not replace water or blood; it confirms them. The Spirit empowers what covenant has established.

Bibliography

1. Theodor J, Albeck C. Midrash Bereshit Rabba: Mit kritischem Apparat und Kommentar. 2nd ed. Jerusalem: Wahrmann Books; 1965.

2. Rice KM. The Noah Generation: The Sign of Revival Rain. Crown City, Ohio, USA: Eternal Kingdom International Publishing, LLC; 2023. 123 p.

3. Rice KM. Cultivating the New Nature: Growing into the Full Stature of Christ. Crown City, Ohio, USA: Eternal Kingdom International Publishing, LLC; 2023. 183 p.

4. Danby Trans. H. Mishnah. Oxford Press; 1933.

5. Ferguson E. Baptism in the Early Church: History, Theology, and Liturgy in the First Five Centuries. Eerdmans; 2009.

6. Neusner J. The Idea of Purity in Ancient Judaism. Brill; 1973.

7. Josephus F. Antiquities of the Jews. Translated by William Whiston. London: W. Whiston; 1737.

8. Reich R. Miqwa'ot (Jewish Ritual Baths) in the Second Temple, Mishnaic and Talmudic Periods. Yad Ben-Zvi Isr Explor Soc. 2013;352.

9. Webb D. Building the Kingdom Through the Local Church. Crown City, Ohio, USA: Eternal Kingdom International Publishing, LLC; 2025.

10. Cohen SJD. The Beginnings of Jewishness. University of California Press; 1999.

11. Neusner J. The Mishnah: A New Translation (J. Neusner, Trans. Yale University Press; 1988. ((Original work published ca. 200 C.E.)).

12. Neusner J. The Tosefta: Translated from the Hebrew with a new introduction. Vols. 1–2. Hendrickson Publishers; 2014. (2nd Ed.).

13. Allen JP. The Ancient Egyptian Texts. Atlanta. SBL Press; 2005.

14. Kramer SN. History Begins at Sumer. University of Pennsylvania Press; 1981.

15. Eliade M. The Sacred and the Profane. Harcourt; 1959.

16. Reynolds JL. Secret Societies. Toronto, Canada: Key Porter Books Limited; 2006.

17. Rite KM. Unchained: Freed to Be His Treasure. Crown City, Ohio, USA: Eternal Kingdom International Publishing, LLC; 2025. 207 p.

18. Keener CS. Acts: An exegetical commentary (vol.3 pp. 2445-2447). Baker Academic; 2012.

19. Livy T. History of Rome. Vol 1 Book 2 B.o. Foster, Trans. Harvard University Press; 1919.

20. Sherwin-White AN. Roman Society and Roman Law in the New Testament. Oxford University Press; 1963.

21. Ehram BD. The Apostolic Fathers. Vol. 1. Harvard University Press. (Didache 7); 2003.

22. Holmes MW. The Apostolic Fathers: Greek texts and English translations. 3rd ed. Baker Academic. (Didache 7); 2007.

23. Meir A. Yitro: Tevilah – Immersion in a Mikveh. Orthodox Union; 2008.

24. n. d. Mikveh: Jewish ritual bath. Biblic Archaeol Soc. 2026 retrieved.

25. n.d. J. In: Encyclopaedia Britannica. 2026.

26. Chisholm H. J. In: Encyclopaedia Britannica. 11th ed. Cambridge University Press; 1911.

27. Duewel WL. Revival Fire: How God can use you to win souls and change hearts. Zondervan; 1988.

28. Edman VR. They Found the Secret. Zondervan; 1956.

29. Finney CG. Lectures on Revivals of Religion. 1835.

30. Liardon R. God's Generals: Why They Succeeded and Why Some Failed. Whitaker House; 1996.

31. Ortlund RCJr. When God Comes to Church: Experiencing Revival Today. Baker Books; 2009.

32. Webb D. Escape the Shame of Babylon. Crown City, Ohio, USA: Eternal Kingdom International Publishing, LLC; 2025. 182 p.

33. Improvement Era. 46(7). Salt Lake City, UT: Improvement Era; 1943.

34. Walker N. Perry Stone protege: Jewel City Revival become the appleof God's eye. Charisma Mag Online. 2022;(April, 5).

Thematic Word Index

317

Scripture Index

Other Good Books
from EKI Publishing

www.ekibooks.com

- *The Unique Factor*
  - By David Webb

- *Escape the Shame of Babylon*
  - By David Webb

- *Building the Kingdom Through the Local Church*
  - By David Webb

- *Building the Temple to Hold the Glory*
  - By David Webb

- *Unchained: Freed to be His Treasure*
  - By Kirkland M. Rite

- *Baptized: Why did I get Wet*
  - By Kirland M. Rite

- *Sozo: What Am I Saved From?*
  - By Kirland M. Rite

Coming from Eternal Kingdom International Publishing

2026

Sozo

By Kirkland M. Rite